Acoustic Masterclass

MIKE DOWLING
Uptown Blues
(American Roots Guitar)

Transcriptions by Mike Dowling and David Hamburger

Photo of El Trovador guitar courtesy of Jeff Vanuga

mikedowling.com

Project Manager: Aaron Stang
Music Editor: Colgan Bryan
Art Layout and Design: Jorge Paredes

© 2004 WARNER BROS. PUBLICATIONS
All Rights Reserved

Any duplication, adaptation or arrangement of the compositions contained in this collection requires the written consent of the Publisher. No part of this book may be photocopied or reproduced in any way without permission. Unauthorized uses are an infringement of the U.S. Copyright Act and are punishable by law.

Preface

This collection of original songs and arrangements offers you a variety of sounds and techniques and, I hope, a few challenges as well. My approach to music is pretty simple. Some things are challenging because of their complexity, while other things can be just as challenging for their very simplicity. My approach to the guitar is to challenge myself to get the most from even the simplest of passages. How can you evoke emotion from the barest of melodies? By having the fundamentals of tone and technique under your fingers and then using these fundamentals to add expression to your playing.

Except for two plectrum compositions called "Backslidin'" and "String Crazy," these tunes are played fingerstyle. I chose them primarily for their range of difficulty. With a little practice, intermediate players should be able to get several tunes under their fingers, and advanced players will find more difficult material to work through as well.

I play several different guitars on the CD that accompanies this book. The guitar that's featured on these pages is my 1933 National El Trovador, my favorite for its warmth, tone, volume, and versatility. I use it for swing as well as blues, and just about everything in between.

I hope you enjoy the tunes, and I'd be flattered if one or two of them make it into your repertoire. Feel free to contact me with questions or comments at mikedowling.com.

Good luck, and I hope you have fun with these songs.

Mike

Contents

Title	Page	CD Track
Preface	2	1
The Compositions	4	
Amazing Grace	14	2
Preview	4	
Bottleneck March	20	3
Preview	4	
Backslidin'	26	4
Preview	5	
Bottomlands	33	5
Preview	6	
Fishin' in the Wind	40	6
Preview	6	
Jan's Song	46	7
Preview	6	
Johnson City Rag	49	8
Preview	7	
Minor Thing	56	9
Preview	8	
Nitpickin'	65	10
Preview	9	
Rocky Road	72	11
Preview	10	
Rosalie	78	12
Preview	10	
Shufflin'	84	13
Preview	11	
Siboney	90	14
Preview	11	
String Crazy	96	15
Preview	12	
Swamp Dog Blues	105	16
Preview	13	
Wild 'Bout It	110	17
Preview	13	
Standard Tuning		18
G Tuning		19
A Tuning		20
D Tuning		21
E Tuning		22
G Minor Tuning		23

The Compositions

Amazing Grace

My E-tuning take on this much-recorded hymn is played with a waltz cadence implied by the thumb fanning across the low strings when the opportunity presents itself. There's not much to preview here. I'm sure the melody is familiar to you, and I've arranged it in a straightforward fashion. Try playing it slowly, taking advantage of the sustain that's available in the open low strings to provide expression.

Bottleneck March

This tune was written as a result of exploring the idea of combining high-register melody notes, either fretted or bottleneck, with open low-register bass notes. That kind of musical spread has always appealed to me. You'll find a variety of fingerpicking techniques in this piece, from forward rolls in the intro to the quirky syncopations in what my wife calls the "cartoon" ending. Some melody notes in the main theme that sound like a pinch (thumb and fingers playing simultaneously) are generated by slides and pull-offs. Practice these passages slowly in order to build up speed for a less frantic sound when you kick up the tempo. The examples that follow are merely exercises and are not taken directly from the song.

Preview
Here's the pinch generated by a pull-off. Repeat slowly until smooth.

Ex. 1

This is a good example of a pinch generated by a slide with your finger. This example isn't from "Bottleneck March," but it's a good one to practice. Repeat slowly.

Ex. 2

Finally, the combination of these techniques:

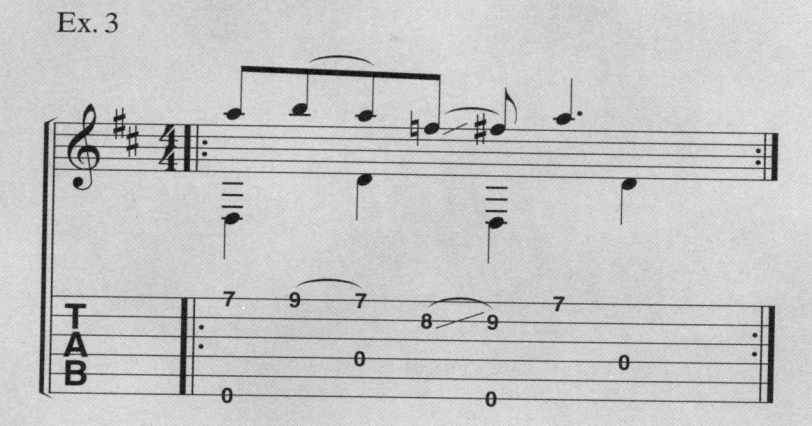

Ex. 3

Backslidin'

This G-tuning bottleneck piece has a kind of quirky bounce to it and is played with a pick. There's a lot of shading to be done with the plectrum, but the chords are laid out in such a way that a miss with your pick won't mean disaster. Instead of designating the up and down picking throughout, I've notated a couple of recurring passages that illustrate my picking pattern. When in doubt, you can always fall back on a strum-like pattern in order to keep the rhythm going, i.e., downstrokes on the beat and upstrokes on the "and"s. You'll see that the song has four parts that repeat with variations. The bottleneck notes are designated as such.

Preview

"Backslidin'" incorporates several diminished 7th chord forms that may be new to you, especially in open G tuning. The Gdim7 in the song introduction (Example 1) is a partially barred and moveable form. The low D7 has no third (Example 2). The high-register D7, along with its accompanying diminished form, is shown in Example 3. As you look at my high D7, notice the chord tones below the chord box. You should be able to get a good visual of how this chord is constructed. The Ddim7 in the next chord box is diminished because you have the flatted 3rd, the flatted 5th, and the double-flatted 7th. Notice how we can go back and forth between the 10th fret D7 and the 9th fret Ddim7 while the top and bottom voices stay the same.

Keep in mind that I wear the bottleneck on my third finger and it will be difficult to play this song if you are accustomed to playing with it on your pinky. Using the third, or ring, finger is a little unorthodox, but if you master the technique, you'll be able to reach some of these underused G-tuning chord forms and you'll be rewarded with fresh sounds to add to your bottleneck bag. Of course this is ultimately your choice. I won't be coming to your house to check up on you, but I encourage my students to at least try it. You might also choose to play the song without using a slide at all.

In Example 4, I call your attention to my fingering for the augmented 7th chord passage beginning at D7 augmented in measure 57. Here I find it helpful to make a partial barre with my middle finger.

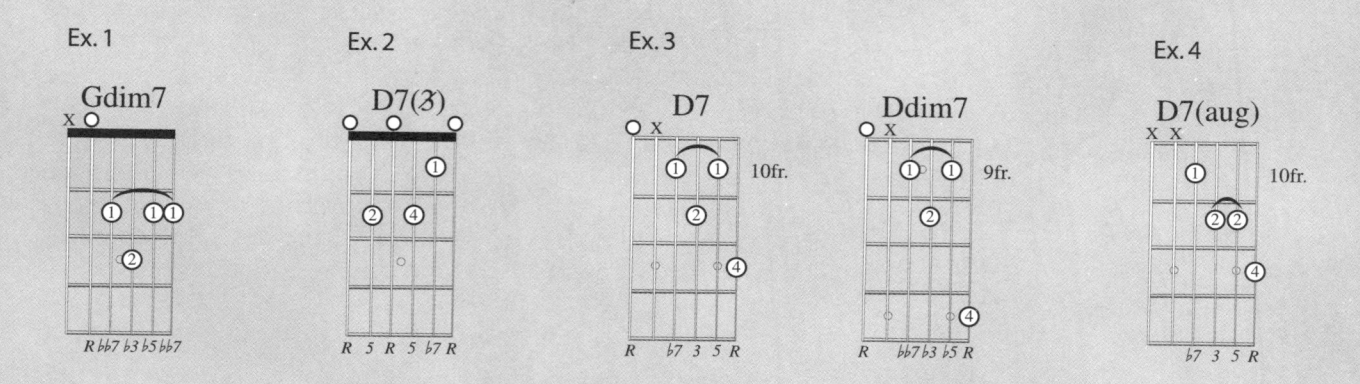

Ex. 1 Ex. 2 Ex. 3 Ex. 4

Gdim7 D7(3) D7 Ddim7 D7(aug)

R bb7 b3 b5 bb7   R 5 R 5 b7 R   R b7 3 5 R   R bb7 b3 b5 R   b7 3 5 R

Bottomlands

"Bottomlands" is a simple slow blues in A tuning that I improvised in the studio over a recurring riff. The riff grounds the tune for me, and for that reason I revisit it at particular intervals. I employ two bass lines in this song. One is a very rudimentary steady, or "dead," thumb. The other is more of an alternating pattern, but not so much as to become the rhythmic focus. The advantage of the dead thumb technique is that it allows nicely for just about any overlying syncopations in the melody. You'll encounter triplets, tied triplet figures for a shuffle rhythm, and even straight eighth notes, while the thumb adheres to its monotonous role. Regarding the attack on your bass notes, when you're confronted with something so simple as quarter notes with your thumb, the challenge is to get the best sound from the guitar. You can either mute the string as you strike it or hit it open and let it ring until it decays. I like to sort of split the difference. I hit it openly in a song like this, and then I bring the heel of my right thumb down on the string to kill it. The result is a clear bass tone with definition and a short decay. The overall feel of the tune is sparse, so in order to bring the song to life, keep in mind fundamental techniques like dynamics, balance, and rhythm.

Fishin' in the Wind

This is my solo version of what was originally a guitar duet I wrote for my *Two of a Kind* CD, recorded with Pat Donohue. This transcription is based on my solo performance from my DVD *Uptown Blues*. This tune is played in a hybrid picking style, using a combination of both fingerpicking and plectrum playing. To do this you hold the flatpick as usual while using your middle and ring fingers to get a fingerpicked, alternating bass sound. The reason for incorporating the pick in this tune is to give a little extra crispness to the bass runs and the other picked passages. Consider the syncopations in this piece to be of medium difficulty. The hardest thing about playing it will be getting used to holding the pick while using your fingers. Try to work through it slowly, and you'll be rewarded in the end with a new technique to add to your bag.

Jan's Song

This is a song I wrote in 1990 for my wife. It takes advantage of open D tonalities, which are easily accessible with very little effort. In other words, it's my kind of song. As in my arrangement of "Amazing Grace," "Jan's Song" is a slow waltz with the thumb implying the three-quarter–time rhythm beneath, but not encroaching on, the melody. Since the melody is so transparent, the notion of getting good single notes with the slide becomes paramount. To achieve this, I try to get definition on my bottleneck notes by employing some right-hand damping techniques. The basic idea is to separate the consecutive slide notes by muting the string between so that the listener doesn't hear me constantly sliding between those notes—unless, of course, you want that sound. I suppose it's a judgment call, but I've always felt that if you master this particular damping technique, you'll have the flexibility of being able to say to yourself, "I'll use a little of it here, or maybe here." To add to this effect, I play "Jan's Song" without picks so that the pads of my bare fingers do the damping. This makes for a nice silent execution of the string muting.

Preview

One of the challenges of using the bottleneck on the third finger is keeping the end of the slide from bumping into the strings when you make your fretted chord forms. It takes some practice to get your third finger to extend enough to keep the bottleneck out of trouble. A slide that's overly long, i.e., longer than what you would need to span your six strings, could make this troublesome for you at first. The slides I use are 2 1/2 inches. Try playing your low fretted G chord and A7 in such a way as to crowd out your third finger so the bottleneck can't sag or fall down onto the strings. When learning these slide techniques, spend a few minutes every day forming the chords with your left hand. You don't even have to play a tune; simply check that you're playing the chord cleanly.

Shown here are my Bm and E7 chord fingerings.

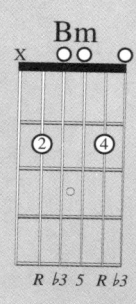

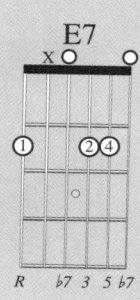

Johnson City Rag

I first performed this ragtime tune in Johnson City, Tennessee. It's in the key of A and has several parts, each affording accompaniment by low-register bass notes. On my CD *Bottomlands* I'm playing with a thumbpick and bare fingers. I like the idea of digging in with my thumb and muting the bass strings for a little more aggressive sound, as opposed to the ringing bass that often gives ragtime guitar pieces an element of staid propriety. But maybe that's just me. In order to articulate the high E7 passage, I used pull-offs while playing an alternating bass. Be patient as you work on this. If you build up speed slowly, you'll find that the tune will come together smoothly.

Preview

As I thought about this tune, the phrase "reading between the lines" came to mind. By this I mean you should be looking at the whole picture, not just the individual notes on the page. The cautionary note here is that very often the notes you're being given are part of bigger chord forms. (See the examples below for using a partial barre to play forms of A and D.) Notice that your fingers are positioned to play optional good-sounding notes beyond what the tune specifically calls for. Taking advantage of opportunities like this is one way fingerpickers can begin to improvise without getting bogged down in scales and theory. There's another advantage to being able to play out of these expanded chord forms—one I've tested several times onstage. As long as you avoid saying "oops" when it happens, you can hit the wrong string and turn the mistake into a save.

Here are some of the chord shapes used in "Johnson City Rag." **Rocky Road**

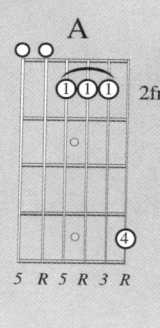

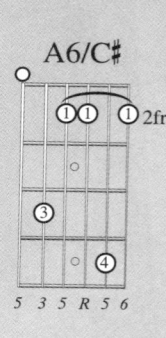

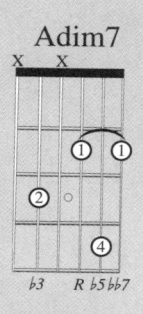

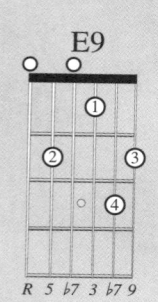

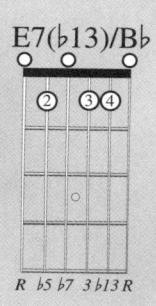

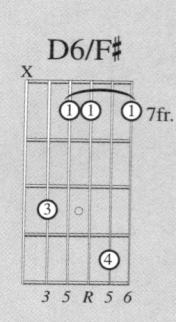

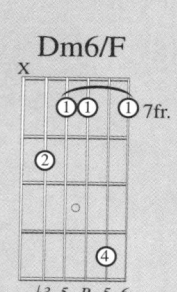

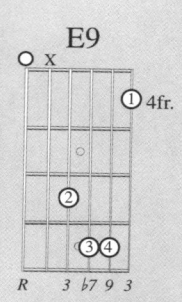

Higher Register

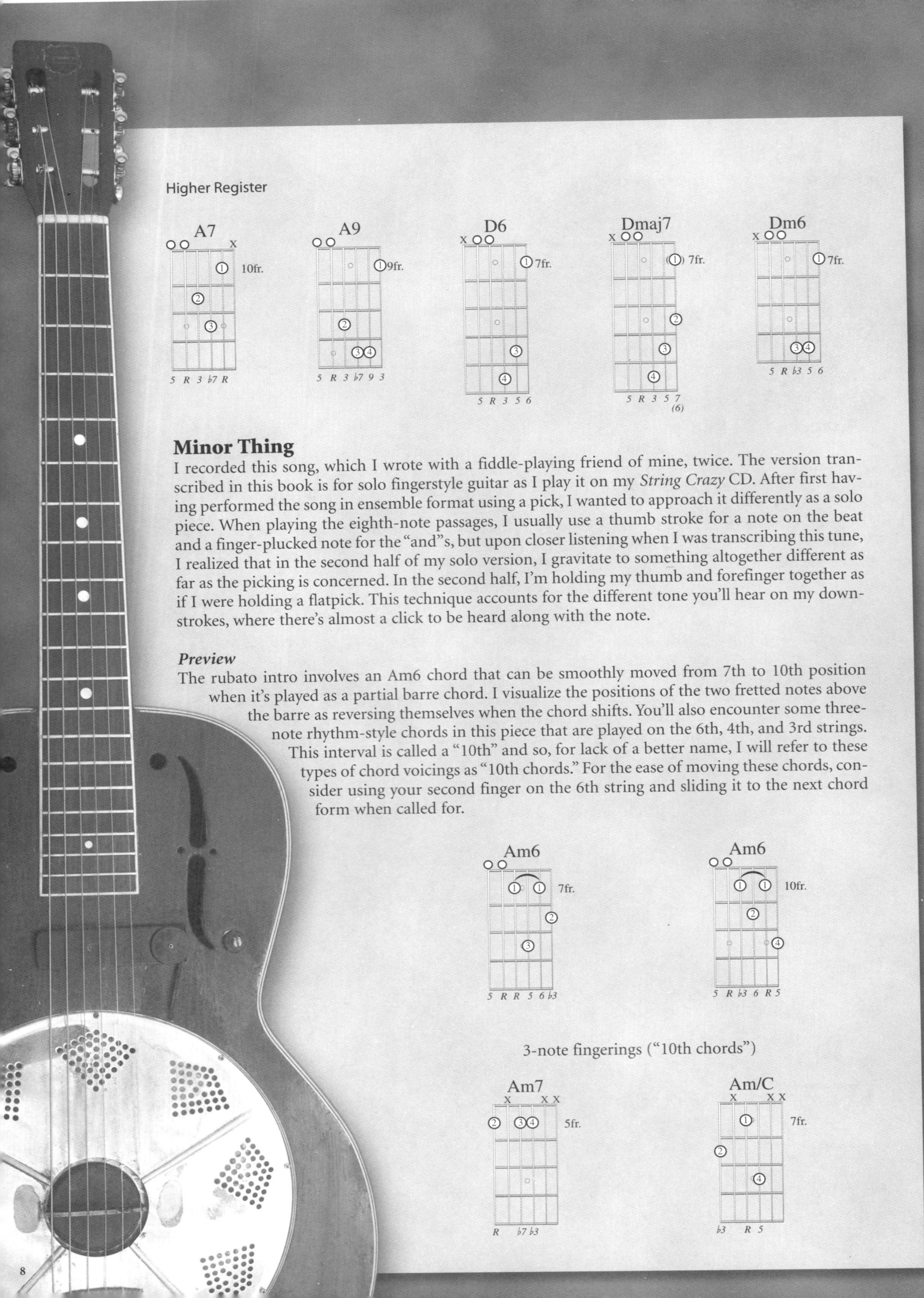

A7	A9	D6	Dmaj7	Dm6
10fr.	9fr.	7fr.	7fr.	7fr.
5 R 3 ♭7 R	5 R 3 ♭7 9 3	5 R 3 5 6	5 R 3 5 7 (6)	5 R ♭3 5 6

Minor Thing

I recorded this song, which I wrote with a fiddle-playing friend of mine, twice. The version transcribed in this book is for solo fingerstyle guitar as I play it on my *String Crazy* CD. After first having performed the song in ensemble format using a pick, I wanted to approach it differently as a solo piece. When playing the eighth-note passages, I usually use a thumb stroke for a note on the beat and a finger-plucked note for the "and"s, but upon closer listening when I was transcribing this tune, I realized that in the second half of my solo version, I gravitate to something altogether different as far as the picking is concerned. In the second half, I'm holding my thumb and forefinger together as if I were holding a flatpick. This technique accounts for the different tone you'll hear on my downstrokes, where there's almost a click to be heard along with the note.

Preview

The rubato intro involves an Am6 chord that can be smoothly moved from 7th to 10th position when it's played as a partial barre chord. I visualize the positions of the two fretted notes above the barre as reversing themselves when the chord shifts. You'll also encounter some three-note rhythm-style chords in this piece that are played on the 6th, 4th, and 3rd strings. This interval is called a "10th" and so, for lack of a better name, I will refer to these types of chord voicings as "10th chords." For the ease of moving these chords, consider using your second finger on the 6th string and sliding it to the next chord form when called for.

Am6	Am6
7fr.	10fr.
5 R R 5 6 ♭3	5 R ♭3 6 R 5

3-note fingerings ("10th chords")

Am7	Am/C
5fr.	7fr.
R ♭7 ♭3	♭3 R 5

Nitpickin'

Mastering this tune will depend on getting what I call a two-against-three syncopation in your right hand. You'll confront this syncopation in the very first passage, and it may remind you somewhat of "In the Mood." Although I describe this syncopation as two-against-three (because the melody notes are grouped in threes), it's really only quarter-note bass against eighth-note melody. It's a good rhythmic motif for guitar players to know, whether you use it in my tune or incorporate it into one of your own. I've transcribed my single string lines in the middle section, and they ought to be played with the thumb striking the notes on the beat and the fingers picking up on the "and"s. This technique, which is certainly not unique to me, will help you keep your rhythm on track. But remember, since the thumb carries more weight to it, you may have to make a conscious effort to keep the thumb from dominating the fingered notes in the single-line passages. I know I do.

Preview
Here are some of the chords you'll need.

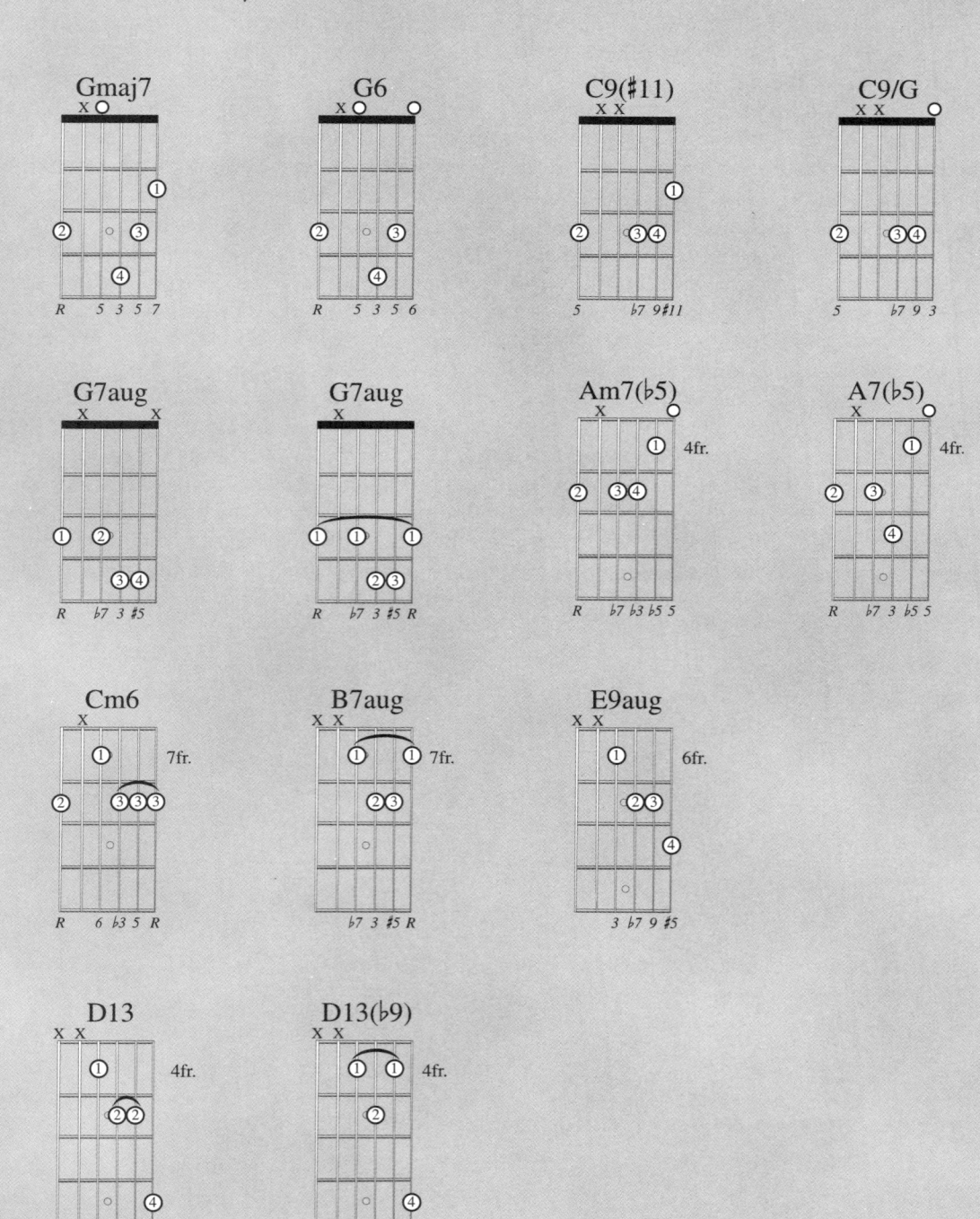

Rocky Road

This is an arrangement of an old gospel tune my friend Bruce Nemerov played for me when he came to visit me in Wyoming a few years back. This song is in D tuning, as is my arrangement of "Hard Times," which evokes a similar mood. My inclination when I encounter tunes with similar sonorities is to go with it rather than try to disavow them. What I'm looking for here is a balance between the old-time sensibility of the original piece and the contemporary chord fragments and backbeat that I've added. If you've already looked at "Rosalie," you'll see that I use the same backbeat slap/brush here but in a very light-fingered manner.

Rosalie

This is my arrangement for solo guitar of a Civil War–era song, "Rosalie, the Prairie Flower," written by George Root. Root wrote other familiar songs of the era, among them "The Battle Cry of Freedom" and "Tramp, Tramp, Tramp, the Boys Are Marching." I learned the basic melody from a friend who in turn had learned it from old piano sheet music he had come across. I arranged "Rosalie" for G tuning, and in the process I slowed it down drastically from what my buddy had played for me, so much so that I felt it needed a little rhythmic resuscitation to keep the song from becoming musically amorphous. I began experimenting with a backbeat and stumbled upon a technique that worked for me. You'll notice I use a similar brush-like backbeat in "Rocky Road." I also wrote an introduction for "Rosalie" using a C minor 6 chord, another somewhat stark departure from mid-1800s pop music. As a composer, I find myself getting as much satisfaction from arranging someone else's music as I do from creating my own, and after years of doing this, I find myself gravitating more toward slower compositions that offer more possibilities for self-expression. For me, it's easier to paint my initials on a slow-moving boxcar than an express train.

Preview

The most challenging part of playing this song is the brush-like backbeat I mentioned above. To achieve this, I brush the strings with my nails and at the same time bring the heel of my right palm down on the lower strings. This happens simultaneously, and if my hand is positioned in front of the sound-hole, my palm can slap the strings against the end of the fingerboard for a more percussive effect. Usually this backbeat occurs between the melody notes; however, there are times when you'll brush to *achieve* a melody note.

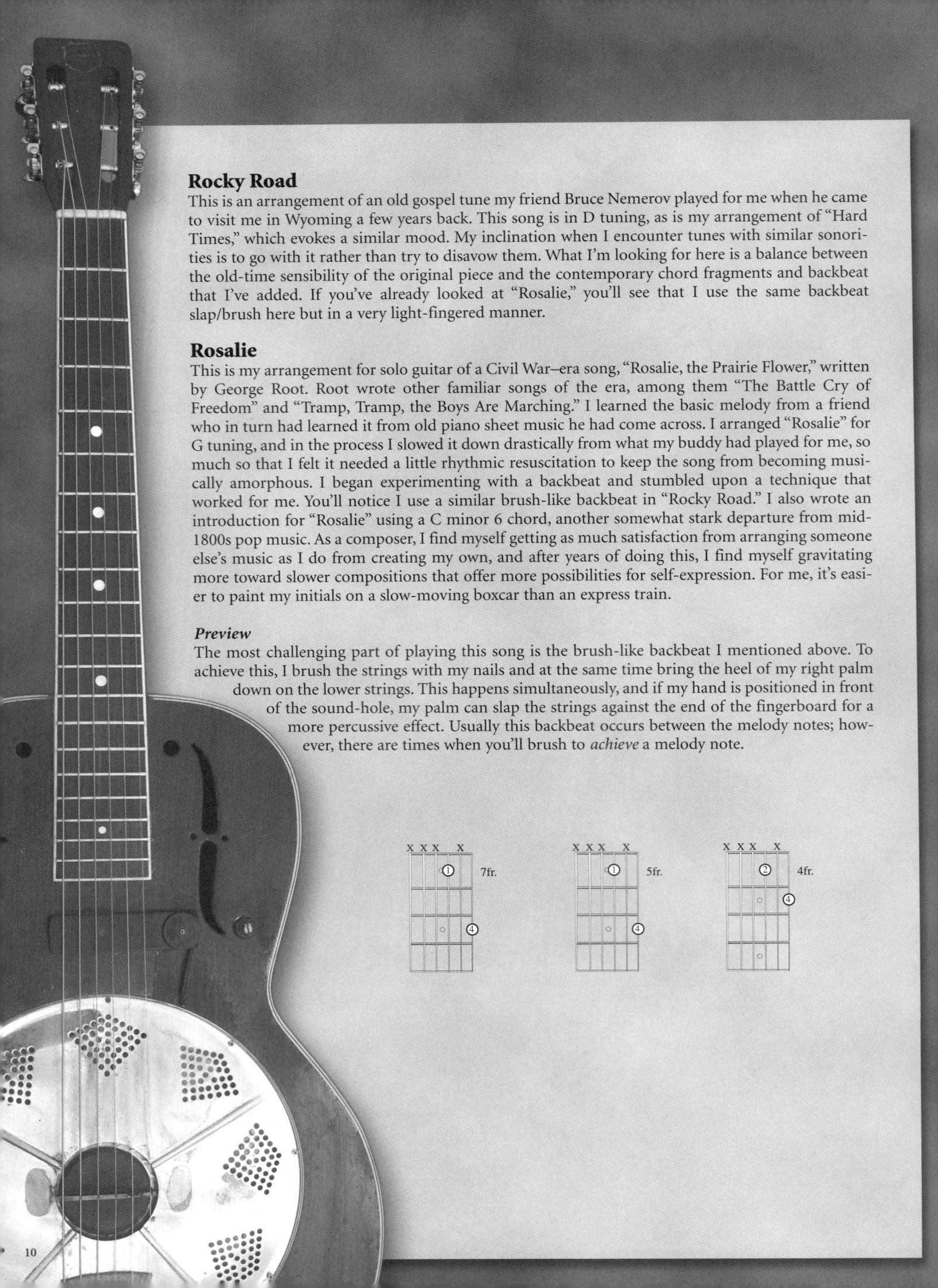

Shufflin'

"Shufflin'" barely qualifies as a slide tune. There's so little slide, in fact, that you could do what there is with your bare finger. It's recorded in E tuning and incorporates a steady bass pattern with common fretted chord patterns in more or less open position. Right-hand damping plays a big part in bringing this song to life, and although the steady bass can begin with a straight muted technique, I'd like you to consider another approach to the bass notes whereby you strike the string and then bring your palm down on it to muffle it. This technique, which is mentioned in the "Bottomlands" preview as well, takes some practice but results in a nice distinct bass note followed by a quick decay, thereby giving the overall sound a nice definition. As you practice this technique, remember to keep your right hand close to the strings so that the off-and-on damping motion of the right heel of your thumb-palm area involves as little motion as possible.

Siboney

Cuban pianist/composer Ernesto Leucona wrote this beautiful song. I'm always listening to "older" music for ideas, and this is one of those haunting melodies that gives me great satisfaction to arrange for solo guitar. Although Leucona employed primarily minor key tonalities, the most compelling passage for me was the one that's played in a major key. When I began fooling around with this piece, I found that I liked it better in a minor tuning with adjustments made to accommodate the section that's played in a major key. This major part I'm talking about is simply a melody with a harmony note placed a third below it. These harmonized pairs sound familiar, but the way they lay out in a minor tuning makes their execution peculiarly tricky. To play them, I find that I need to put my usual fretboard instincts into a sort of mental override and rely instead on memorization. When you try it, you'll see what I mean.

Preview

Your main task in mastering this piece is memorization. Although these chord forms in G-minor tuning may be new to you, they're rather simple to make. For the ease of playing the major key part that involves the two-note pairs, you'll see my preferred fingerings. The paired notes at the same fret (Example 1) are to be played with the third and fourth fingers, and the other pairs, separated by one fret (Example 2), are fingered with the second and fourth fingers. Practice these fingerings slowly at first.

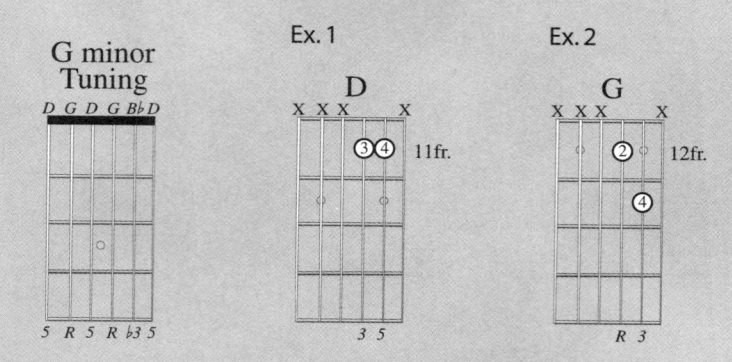

Here are the other main chords for "Siboney."

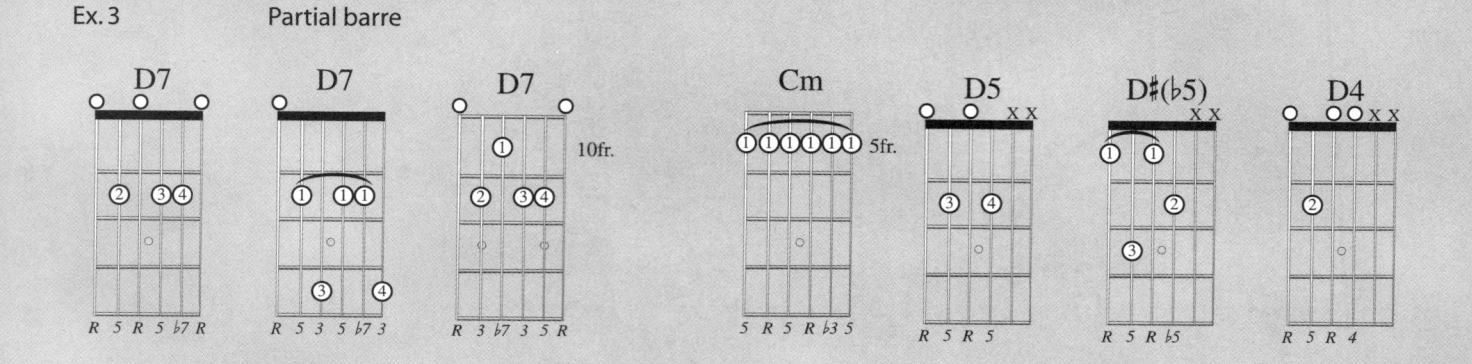

String Crazy

This tune follows a simple western swing-like progression and has as its theme a series of ornamented three-note close-voiced chords that were inspired by a fiddle riff. There are two choruses to follow in sort of a rhythmic 1930s chord solo style. You'll encounter some "x"ed out chords that supply some syncopation.

Preview

It's important to keep your right hand in a down-up motion to capture the syncopated nature of the riff. It will take some practice. Example 1 below shows the basic syncopation and the location of the accents in the up-down picking scheme without ornamentation. Note that all eight down and up symbols are represented and that those in parentheses are omitted, but you should keep the right hand moving anyway.

Ex. 1

Example 2 illustrates the syncopations along with the chord position.

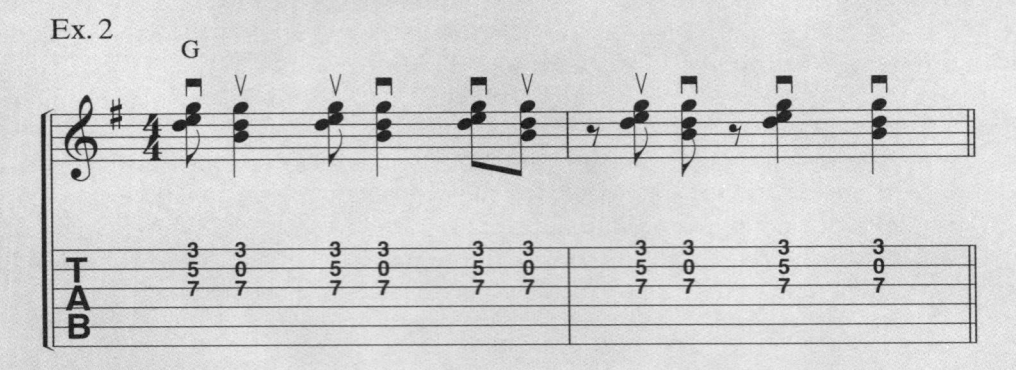

Ex. 2

Example 3 is simply the pull-off and the hammer-on on the B string.

Ex. 3

Example 4 puts it all together to complete the riff.

Ex. 4

Swamp Dog Blues

Sliding around in open tunings is one of the most accessible ways to create expressive, compelling music. This observation is certainly not unique to me and it's why slide playing became so popular in the first place. What I like about these tunings for bottleneck guitar is the way the open low strings can support the overlying melody to provide the effect of a self-accompaniment. I wrote "Swamp Dog Blues" in open D with this in mind. You'll hear this technique in the opening phrase where the open low strings lend support to a single slide line as its played on the 1st string.

Of course, with the melody exposed like this you'll need to make sure your slide notes are as solid as you can make them. There's nothing in particular you need to preview, but your focus should be on intonation, vibrato if you choose to use it, and getting a balance between your slide notes and the fretted tones that both make up the melody. I've indicated which passages are played with the slide and which are played with the fingers.

I sometimes incorporate a pull-off with my bottleneck, usually from the 2nd fret, 1st string, to an open 1st string. In order to achieve this effect, experiment with easing the slide down and off the string. Remember, I wear the bottleneck on my ring finger, and if you haven't tried this technique, this would be a good tune to practice it on. I find I can better control the slide, and therefore the vibrato, with the bottleneck bracketed between my middle and little fingers. This might sound like a picky admonition to do as I do, but there are no hard and fast rules for slide playing. I'm just encouraging you to at least try it. Heck, Hound Dog Taylor had six fingers on his slide hand. And you thought *you* had a decision to make.

Wild 'Bout It

This is a song based on a simple riff, and I've transcribed it as it was improvised in the studio. It's in E tuning and it's played without the bottleneck, although there are many slide-like passages. I use fundamental techniques here like sliding on the string with my finger(s), hammering on, and pulling off to add expression to my fretted passages. This song is basically a 12-bar blues, but it is written in a 24-bar form because of the cut-time feel and to make it easier to read. You'll notice that I incorporated an A9th chord that has a low root. This gives the player some nice possibilities for fingerpicking. Since there aren't many options for a full-sounding IV chord with a root in the bass, I hope this shape will find its way into your chord vocabulary for E and also D tuning.

Preview
These are the chord forms you'll encounter in "Wild 'Bout It."

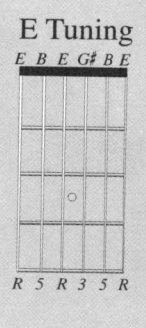

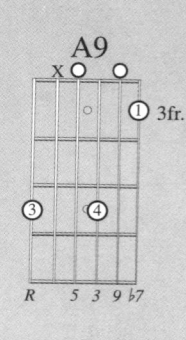

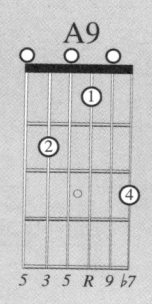

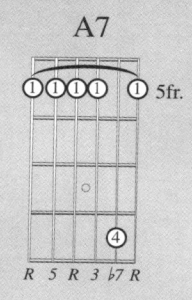

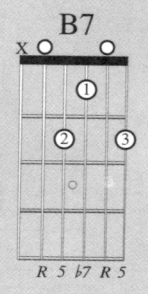

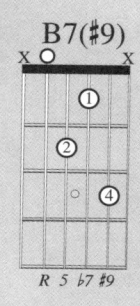

Amazing Grace

Traditional
Arranged by MIKE DOWLING

Open E tuning:
⑥ = E ③ = G#
⑤ = B ② = B
④ = E ① = E

let ring throughout

*Brush with back of right-hand fingernails to produce a percussive backbeat.

Amazing Grace - 6 - 2
SAIR007

16

Amazing Grace - 6 - 3
SAIR007

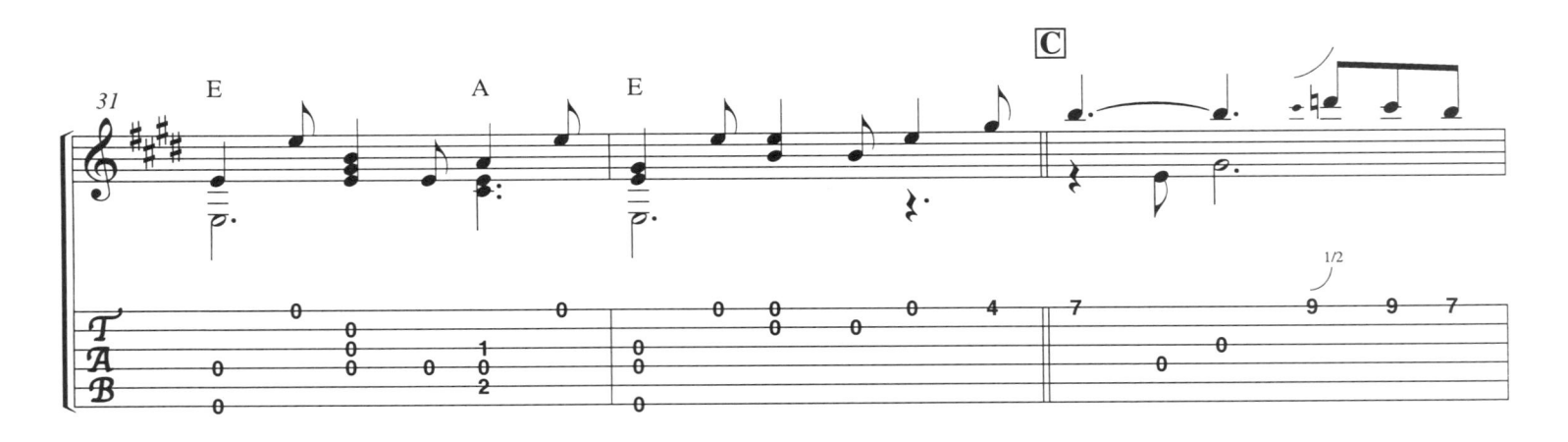

17

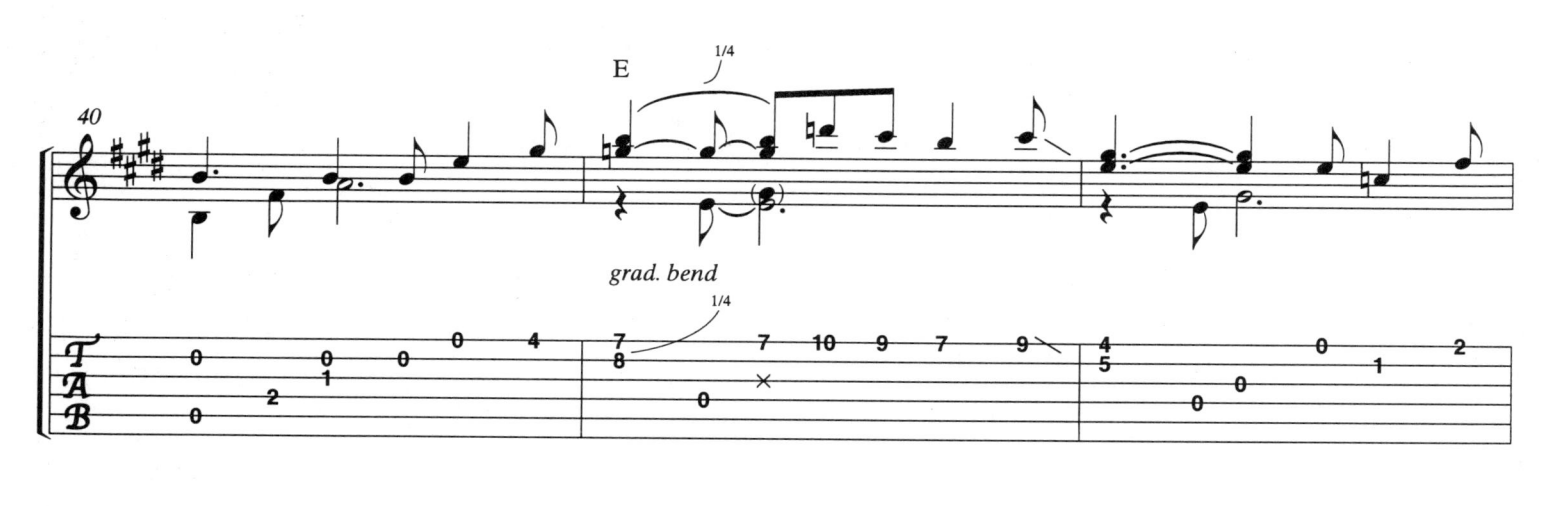

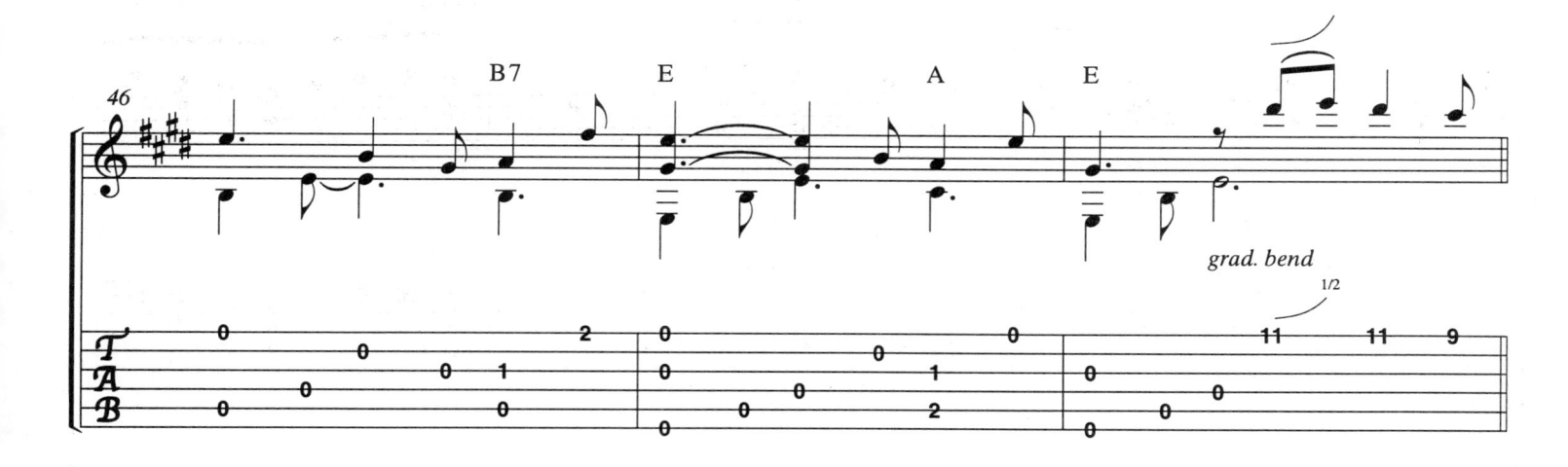

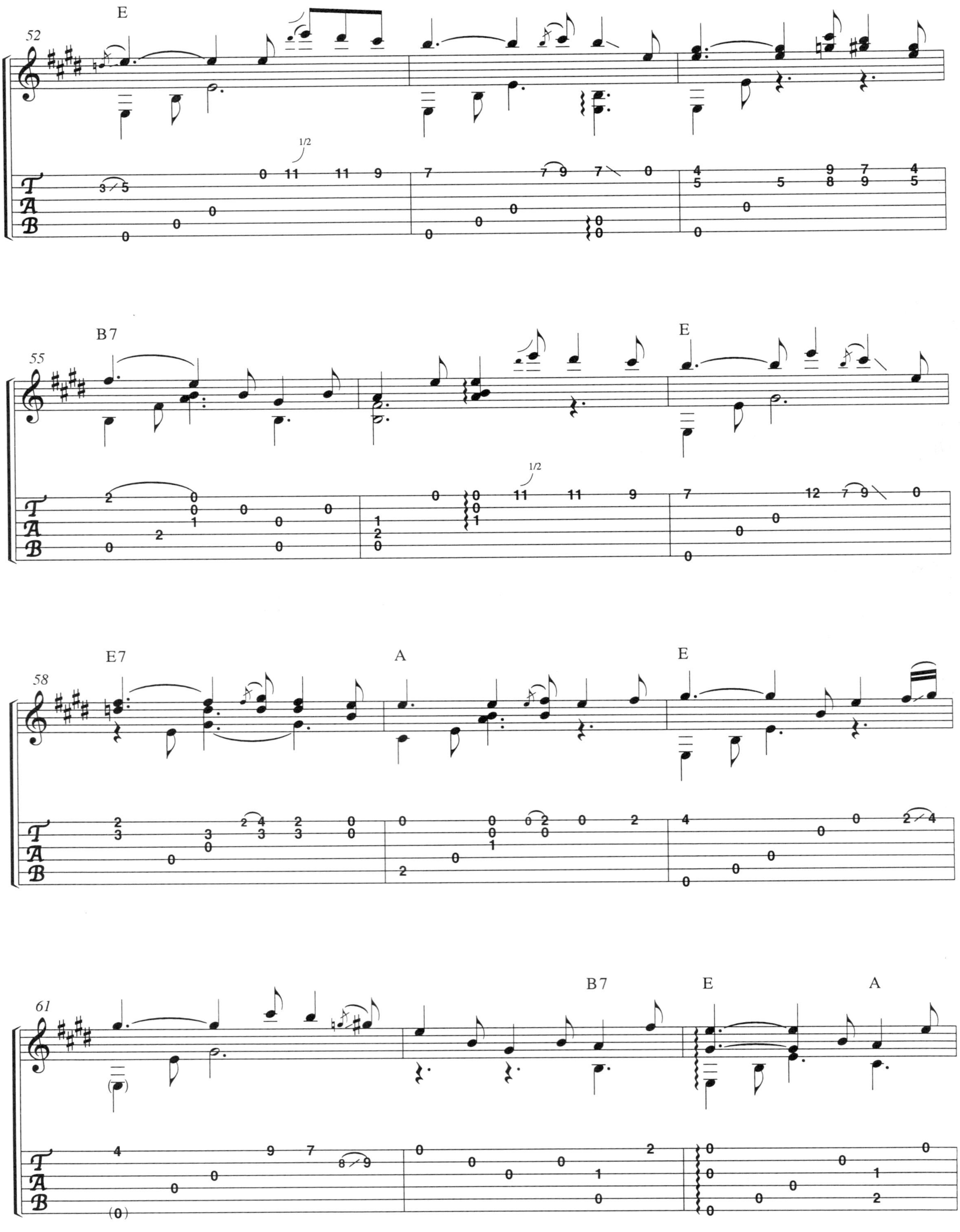
52
E
1/2
55
B7
E
1/2
58
E7
A
E
61
B7
E
A

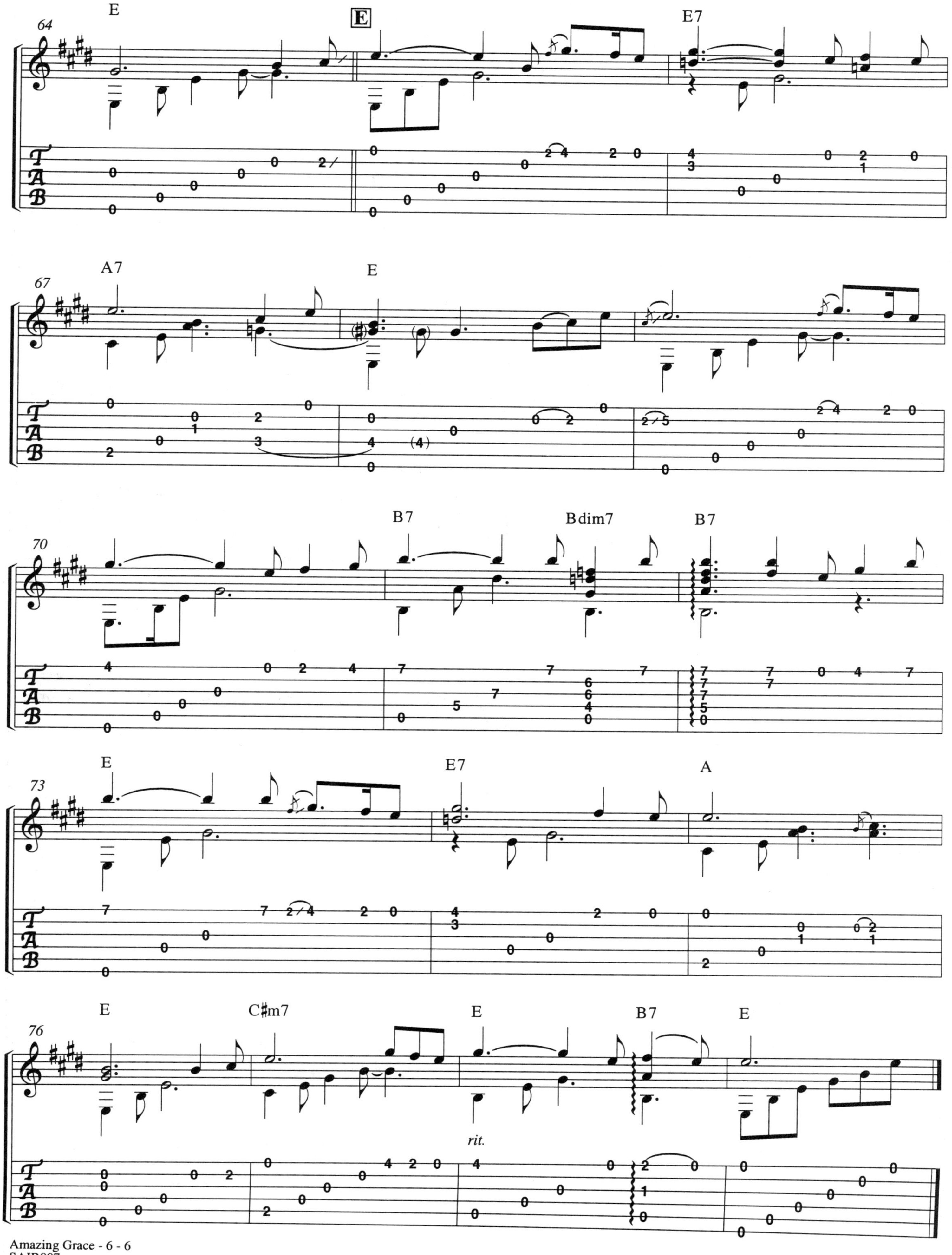
64
E
E
E7
T
A
B
67
A7
E
70
B7
Bdim7
B7
73
E
E7
A
76
E
C♯m7
E
B7
E
rit.

Bottleneck March

By MIKE DOWLING

Open D tuning (w/slide):
⑥ = D   ③ = F#
⑤ = A   ② = A
④ = D   ① = D

Moderately fast

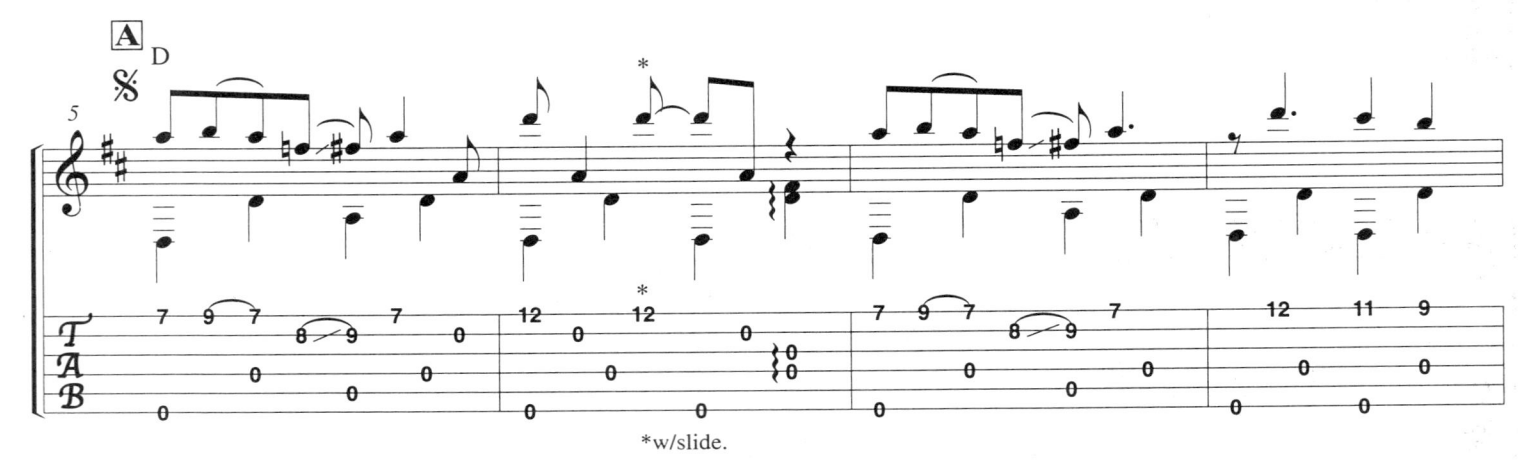

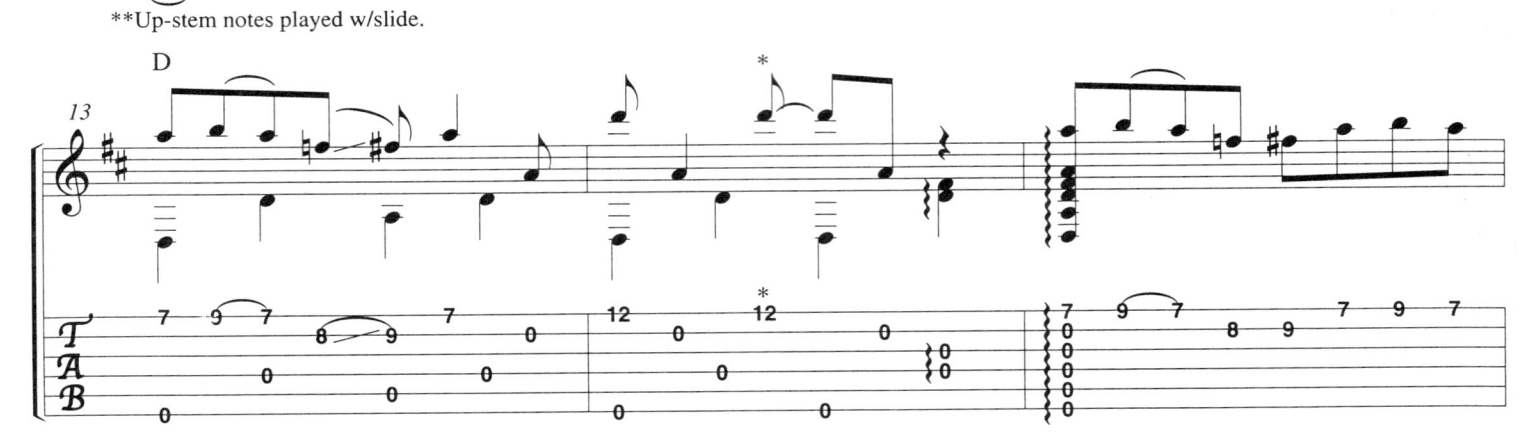

*w/slide.

**Up-stem notes played w/slide.

Bottleneck March - 6 - 1
SAIR007

© 1991 TableTop Music (ASCAP) and Solid Air Music (ASCAP)
All Rights Reserved

To Coda
16
A
w/slide
19
D
B
D
harm.
23
D
A7
1.
harm.
27
D
2.
30
D
C
B♭
B♭
w/slide

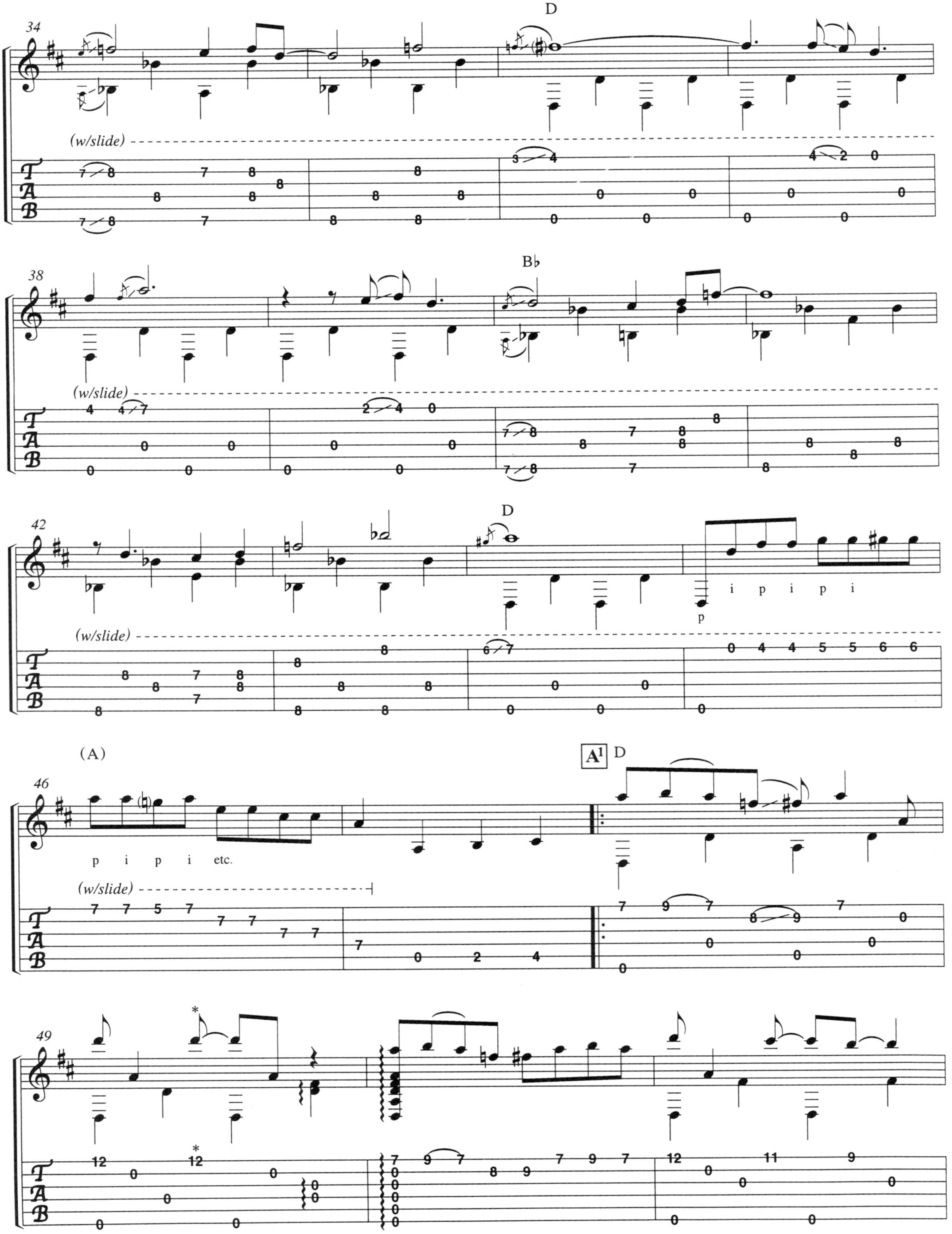
D
(w/slide)
B♭
(w/slide)
D
i p i p i
p
(w/slide)
(A)
A1 D
p i p i etc.
(w/slide)
*
*

1. A
w/slide
2. A
D
w/slide
N.C.
p i m p i m etc.
D
D
p i p i m p m p
B♭ A
w/slide
D
m i p i m p i m p p i m p i p i
w/slide

D
71
p i p i m p
p i p i
(w/slide)
B♭ A
D
75
p i p i
m i p i m p i m
w/slide
E
A7
78
D
82
A7
w/slide
D
85
A7

*Place slide between nut & first fret with harmonic still ringing & slide up to 12th fret.

Backslidin'

By MIKE DOWLING

Open G tuning:
⑥ = D   ③ = G
⑤ = G   ② = B
④ = D   ① = D

Moderate shuffle (♫ = ♩♪)

plectrum style

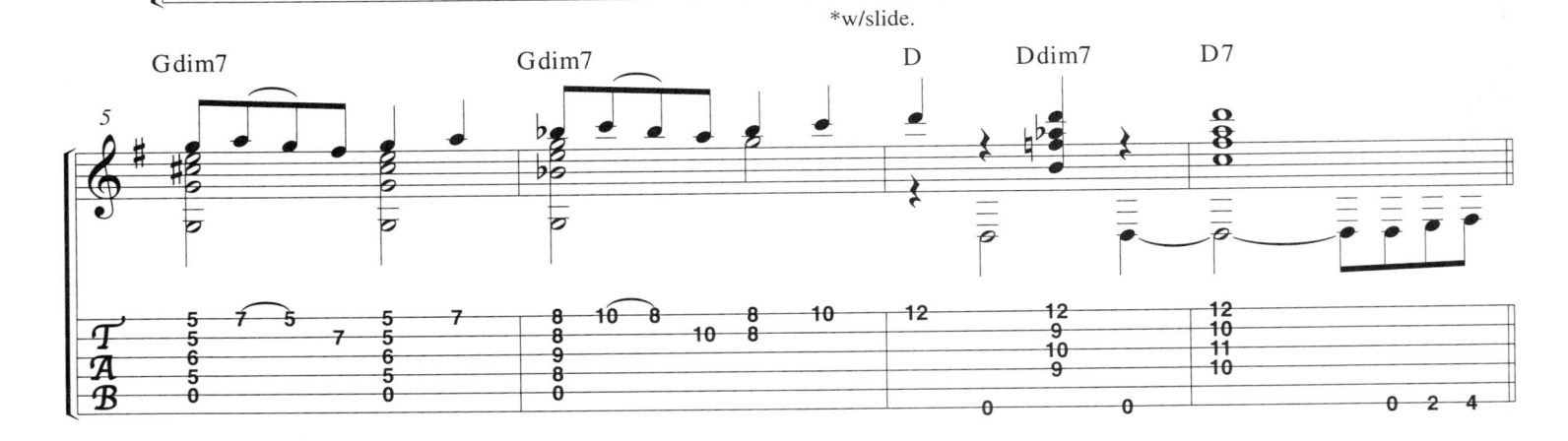

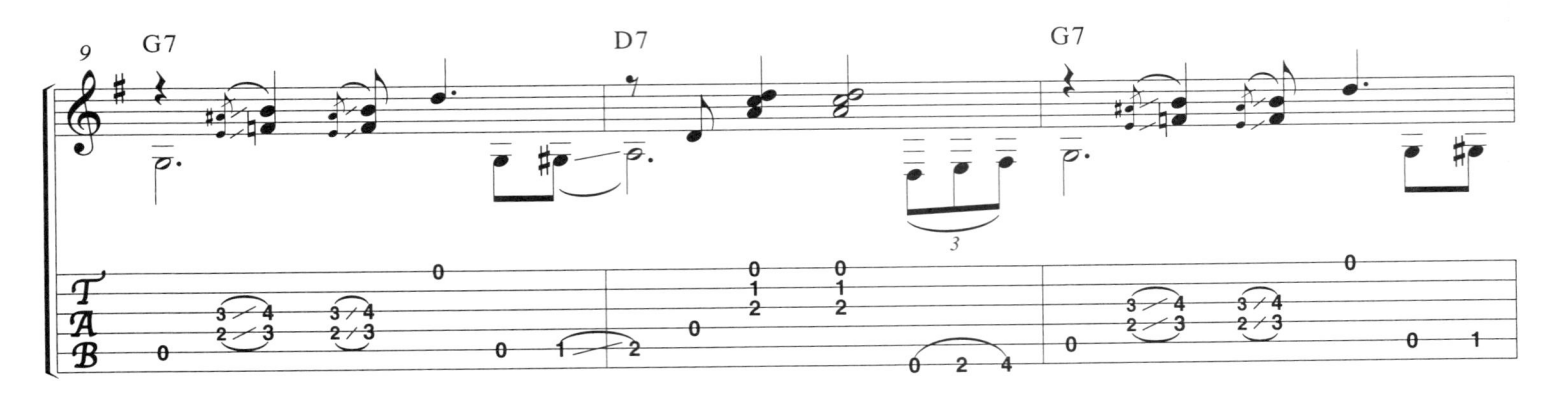

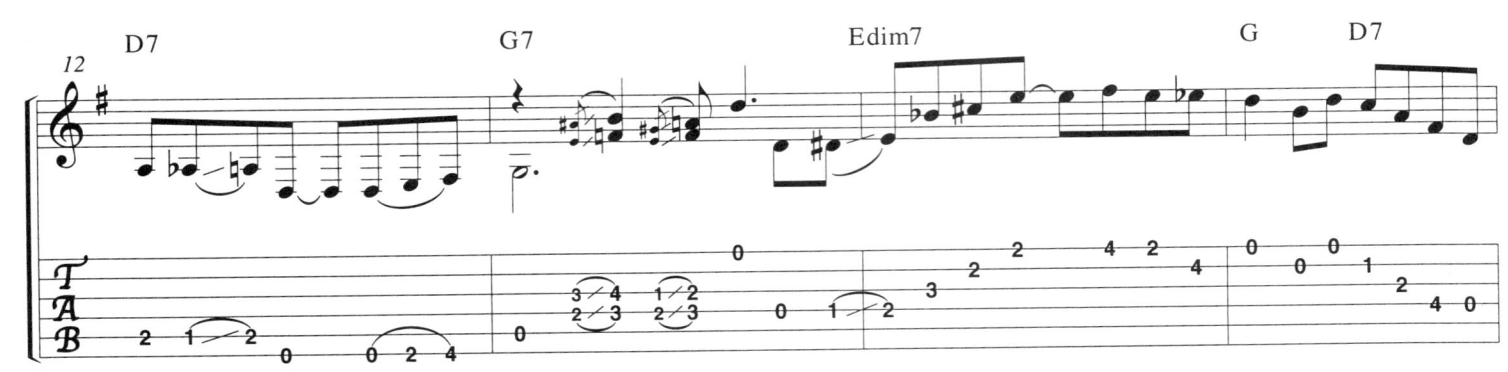

*w/slide.

Backslidin' - 7 - 1
SAIR007

© 1995 TableTop Music (ASCAP) and Solid Air Music (ASCAP)
All Rights Reserved

27

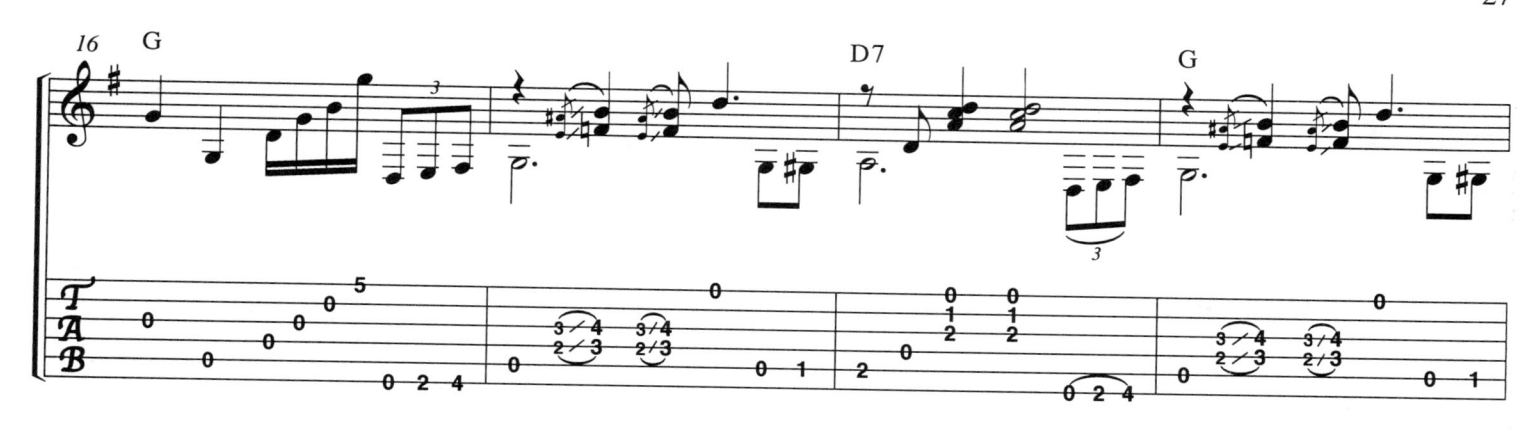

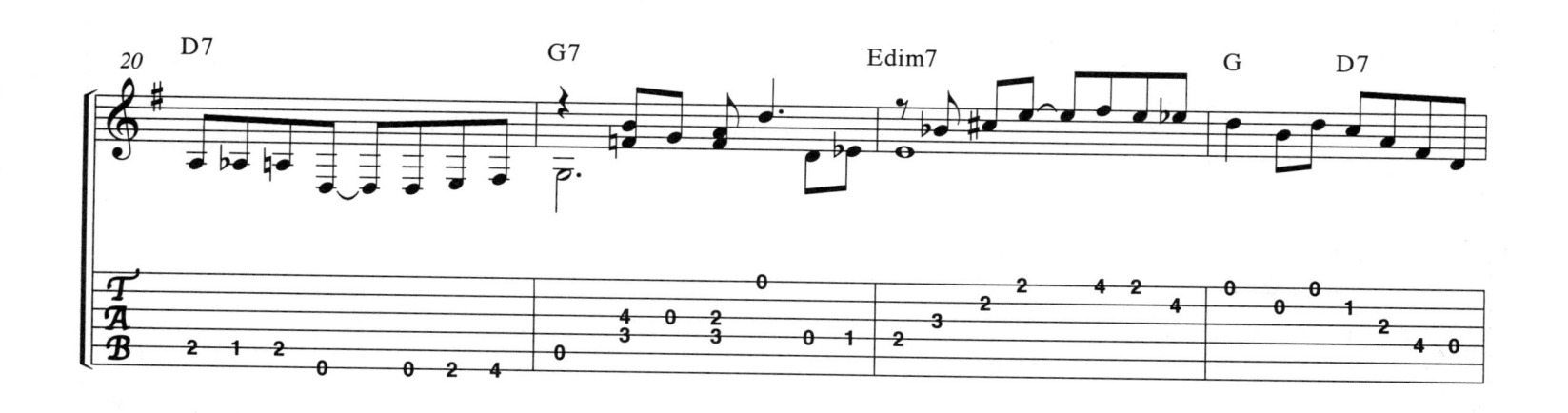

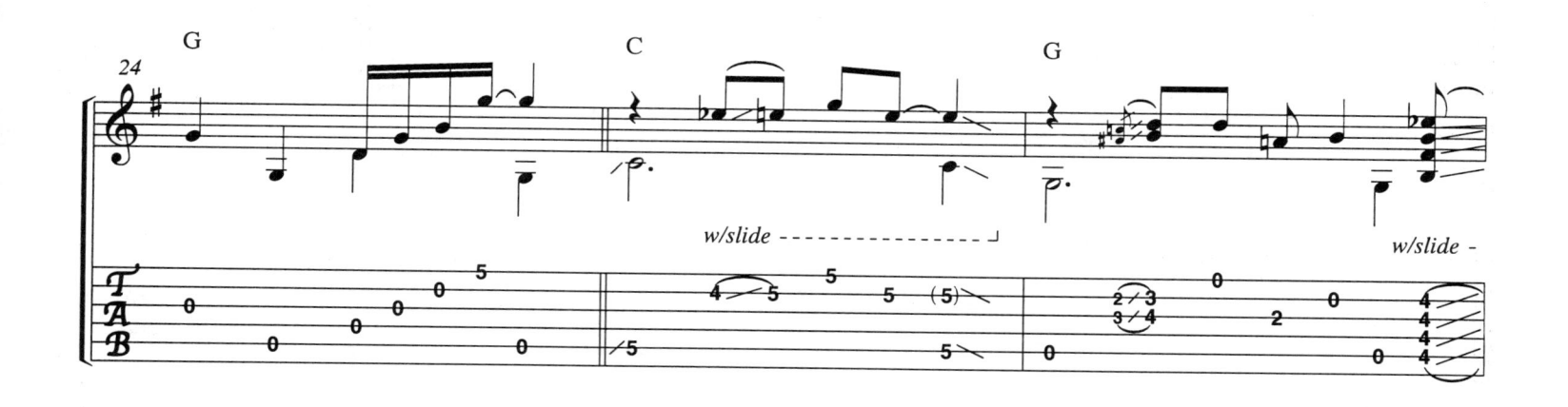

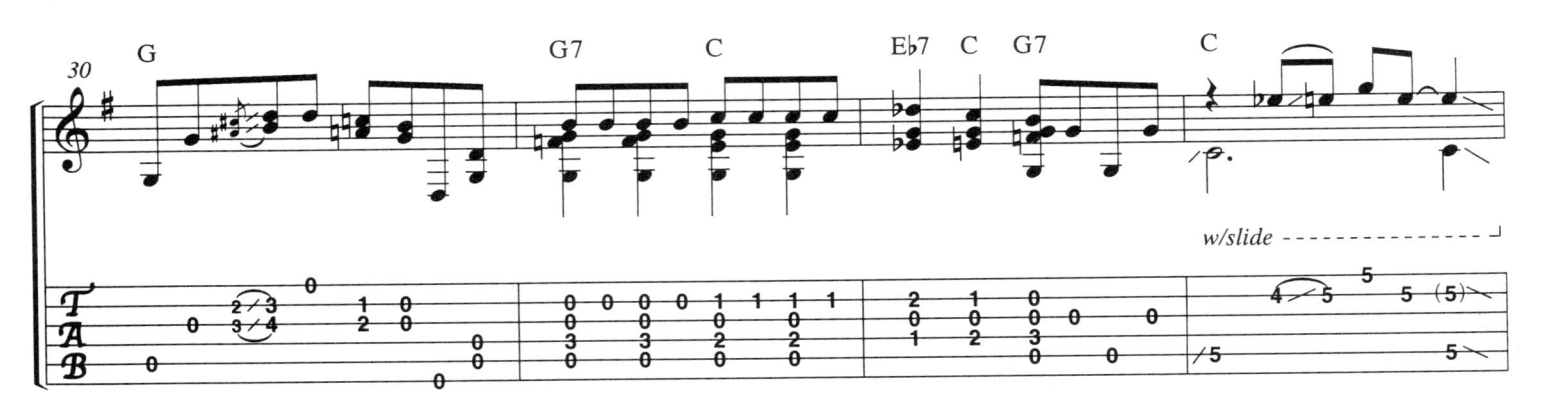

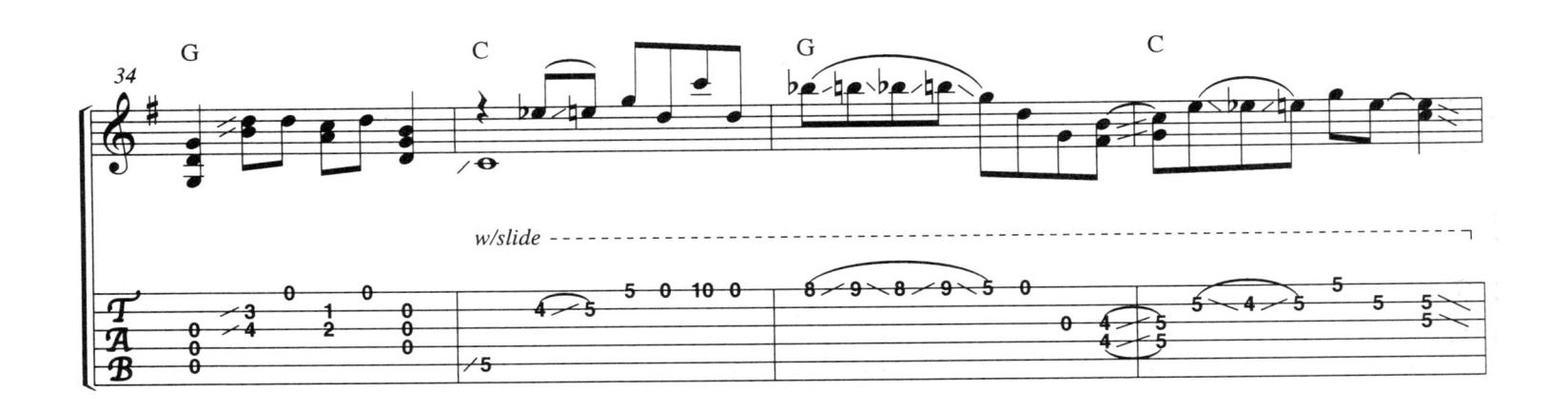

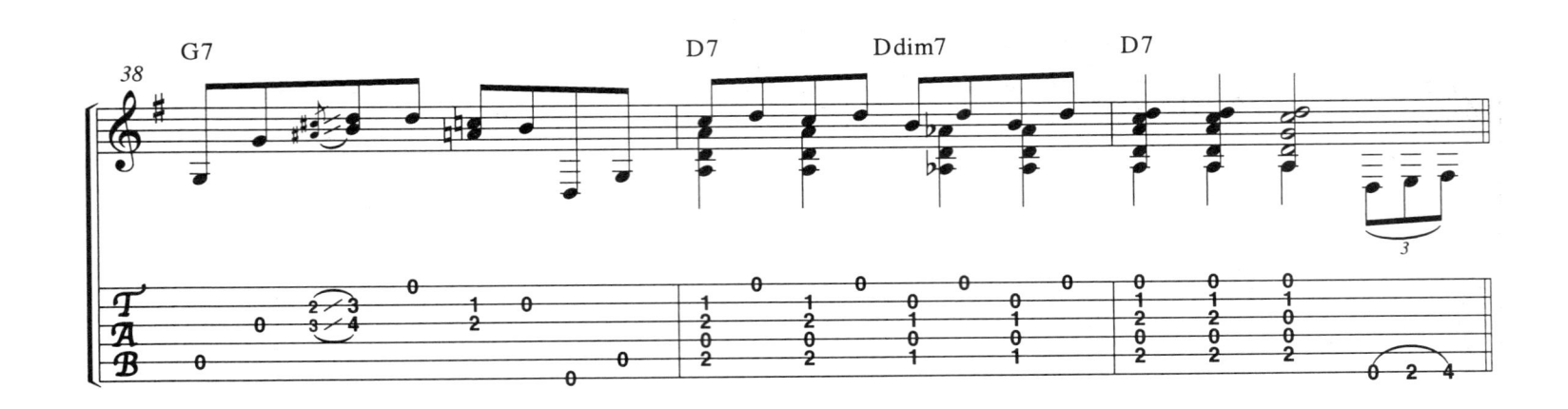

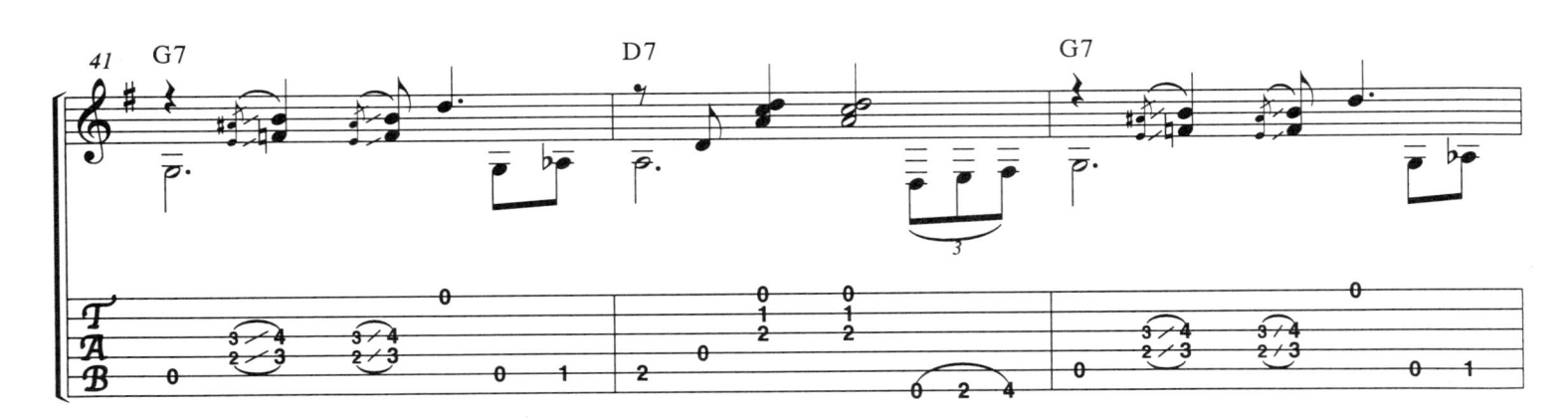

Backslidin' - 7 - 3

44
D7
G7
Edim7
G
D7
48
G
Gdim7
G
Gdim7
*w/slide.
52
G
Gdim7
w/slide
D
Ddim7
56
D7
Ddim7
D7(♯5)
C7(♯5)
B♭7(♯5)
A♭7(♯5)
F♯7(♯5)
A♭7(♯5)
B♭7(♯5)
C7(♯5)

59
D7(♯5)
G
D7
harm.
63
G
D7
G
66
Edim7
G
D7
G
G7
70
D7
G
D7
G7
74
Edim7
G
D7
G
C
w/slide

31

Backslidin' - 7 - 6
SAIR007

94
D7
G
D7
G
98
Edim7
G
D7
G
Gdim7
102
G
Gdim7
G
Gdim7
w/slide
w/slide
106
D
D7
G
w/slide
*gradual slide
*w/o slide.

Bottomlands

By MIKE DOWLING

Open A tuning:
⑥ = E   ③ = A
⑤ = A   ② = C#
④ = E   ① = E

Slow blues

*Brush with back of right-hand fingernails to produce a percussive backbeat.

Bottomlands - 7 - 1
SAIR007

© 2001 TableTop Music (ASCAP) and Solid Air Music (ASCAP)
All Rights Reserved

E7
A9
B
straight 8th notes
Cdim
Bdim
A9
(straight 8th notes)
D7
straight 8th notes
A7
E7

35

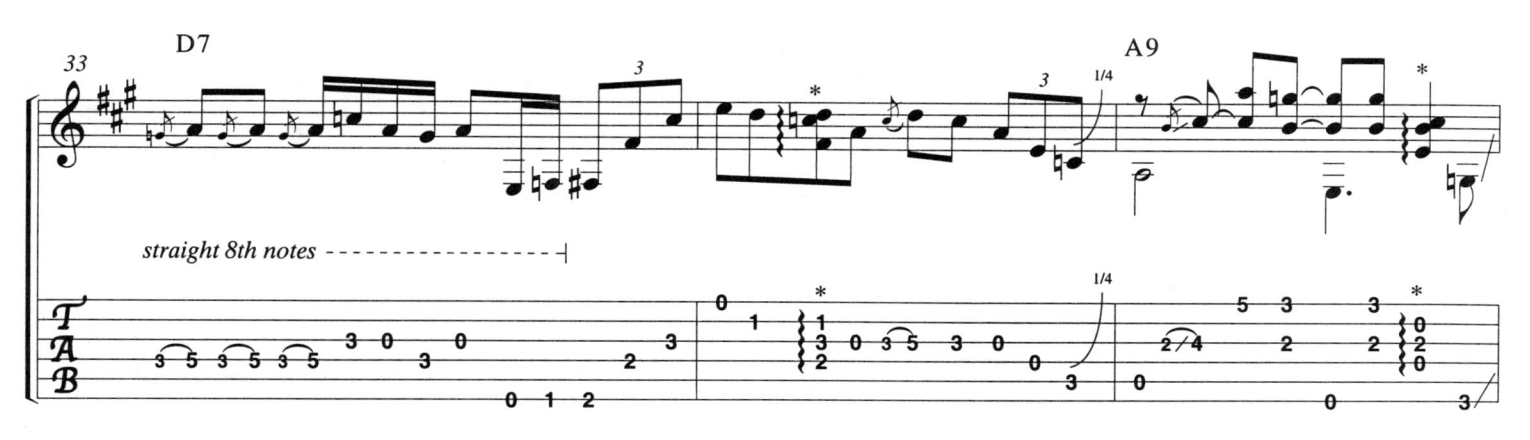

36
E7
straight 8th notes
39
A9
D
*Tremolo w/middle finger.
42
Cdim
Bdim
A7
E7
A7
straight 8th notes
45
D7
A7
E7
*Brush w/fingernails.

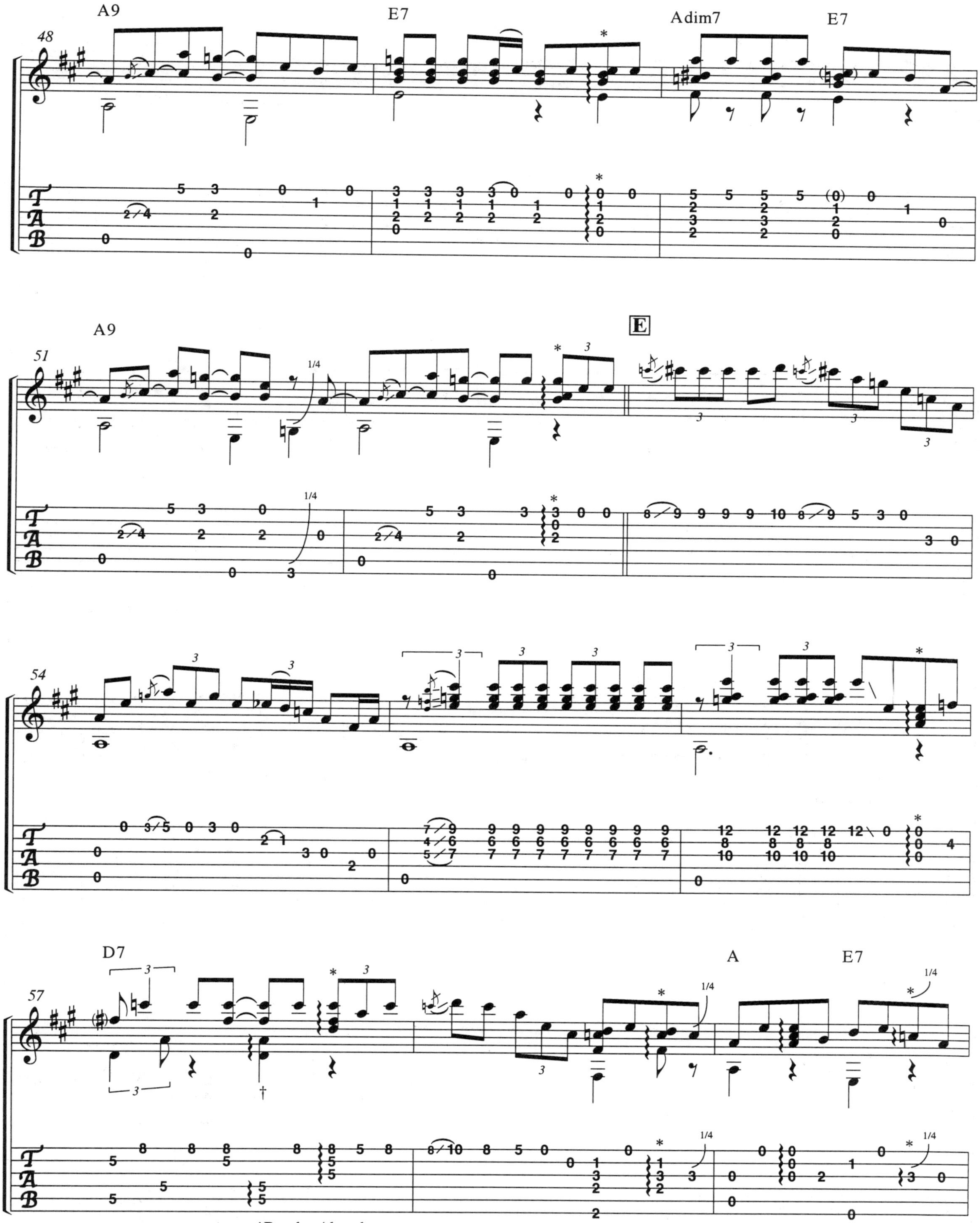

†Brush w/thumb.

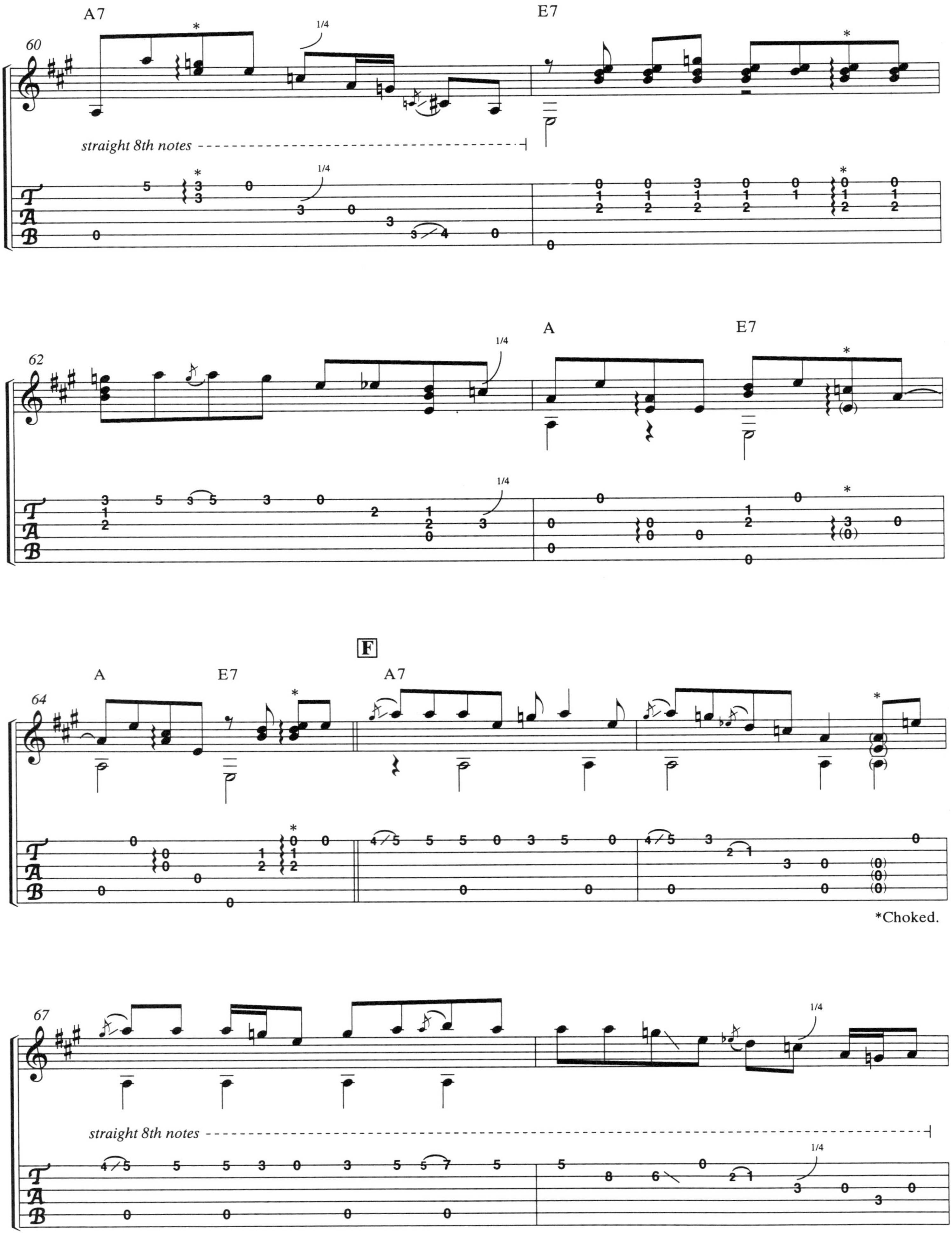
A7
E7
straight 8th notes
60
62
A
E7
F
64
A7
67
*Choked.

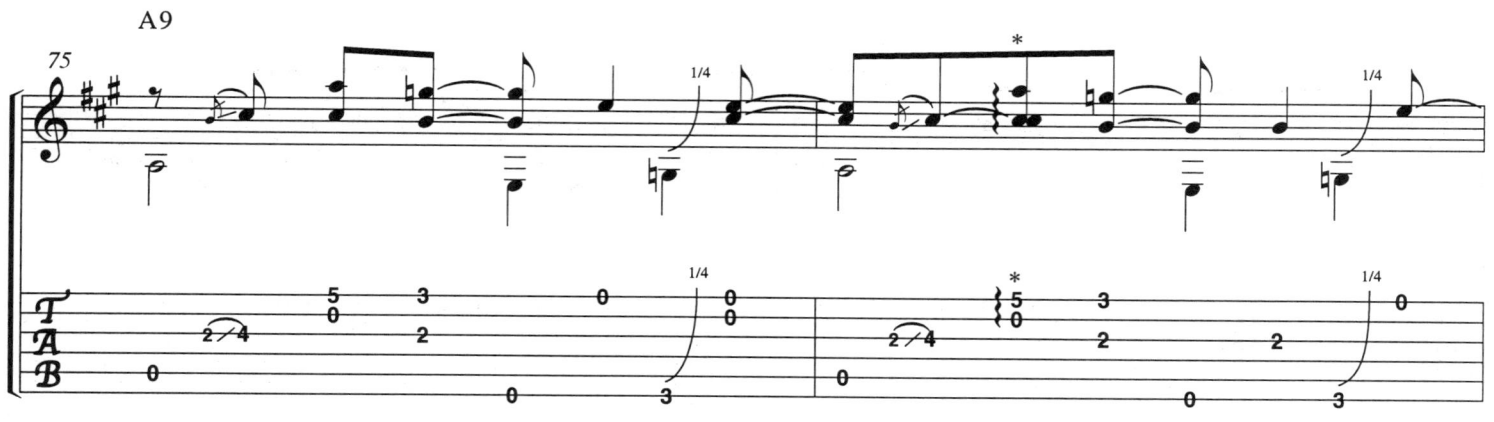

Bottomlands

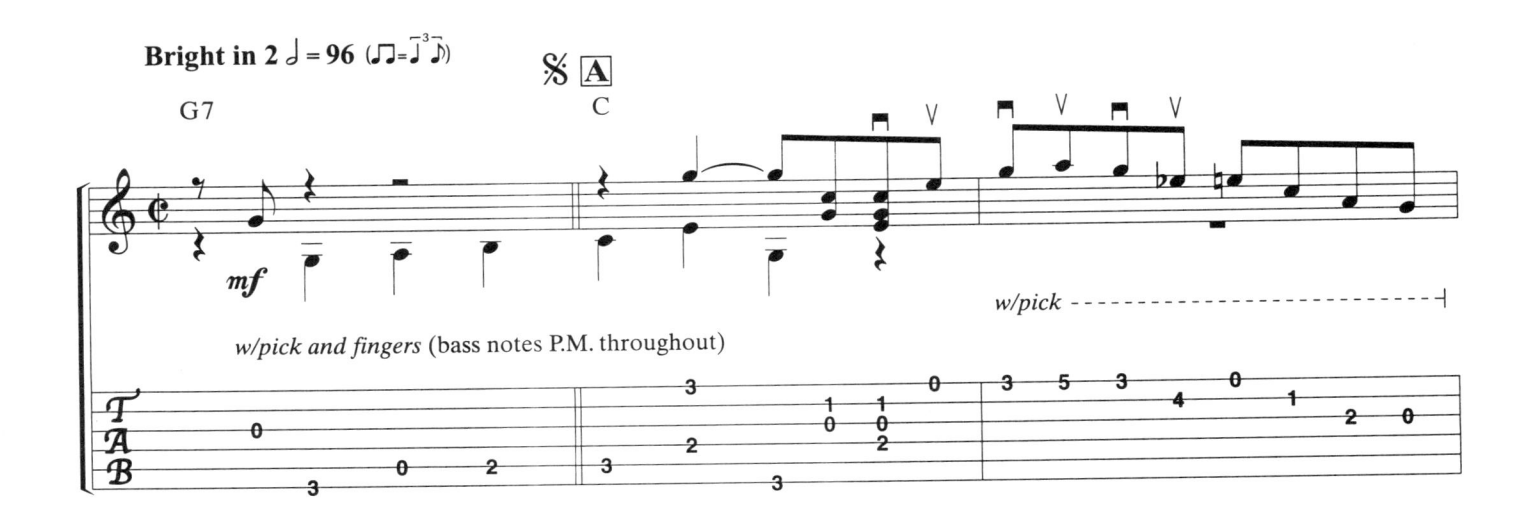

Fishin' in the Wind

By MIKE DOWLING

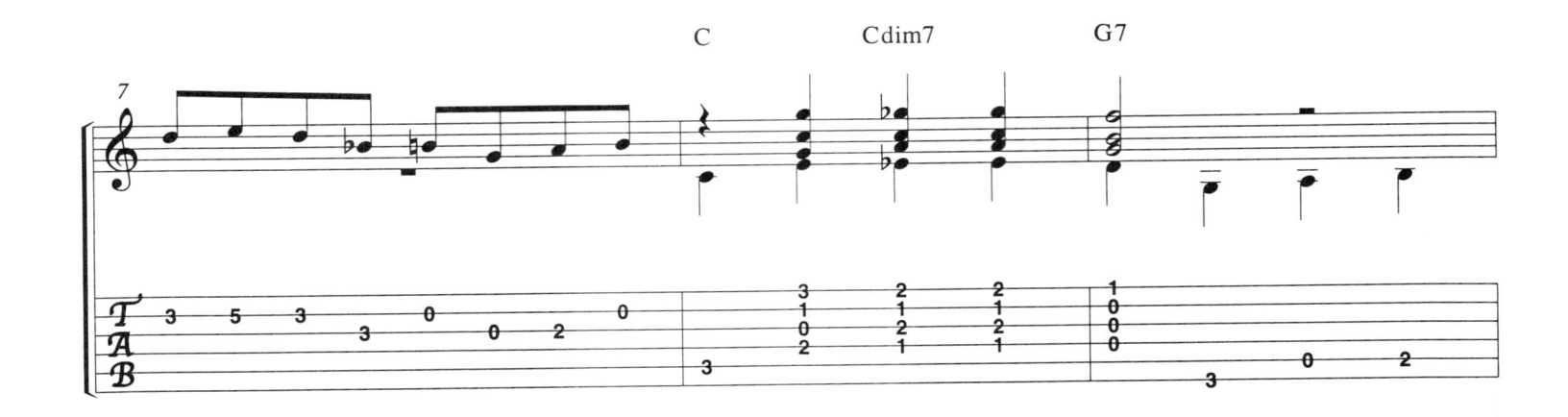

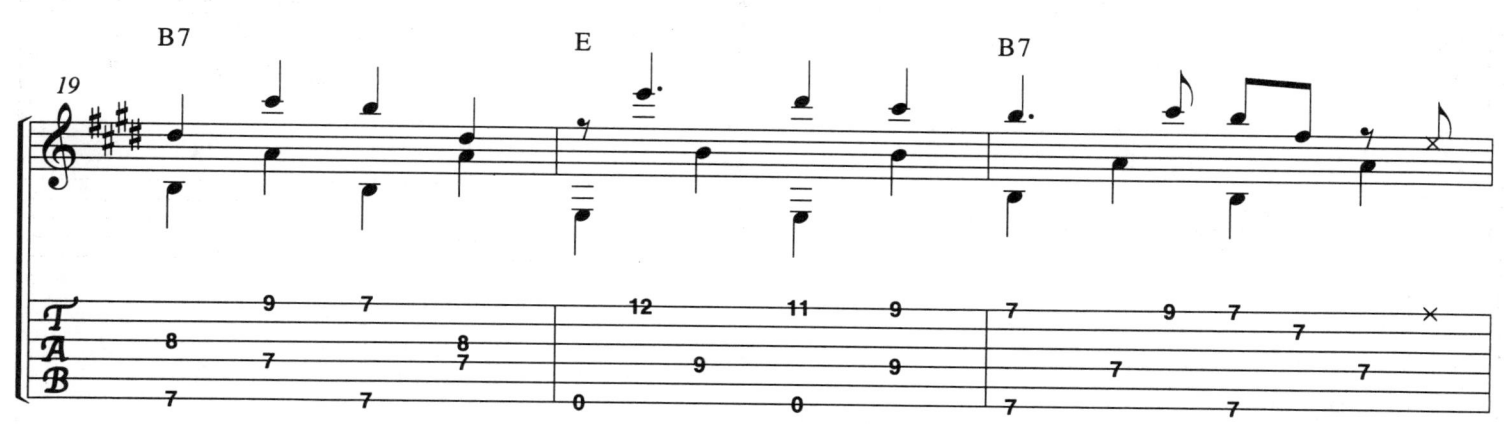

Fishin' in the Wind - 6 - 2

42

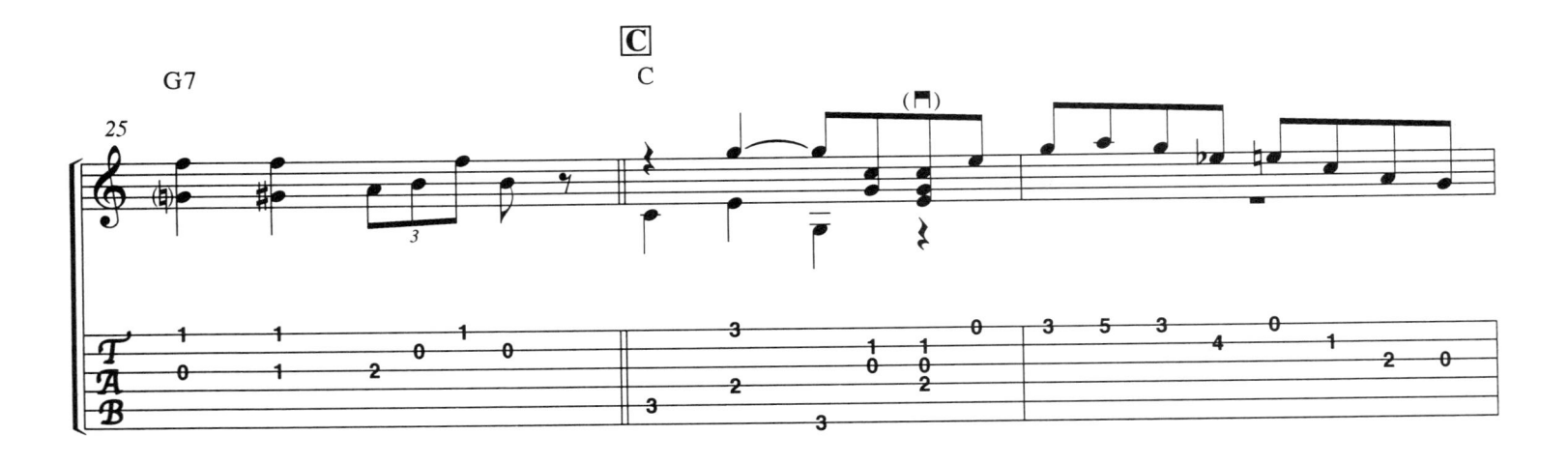

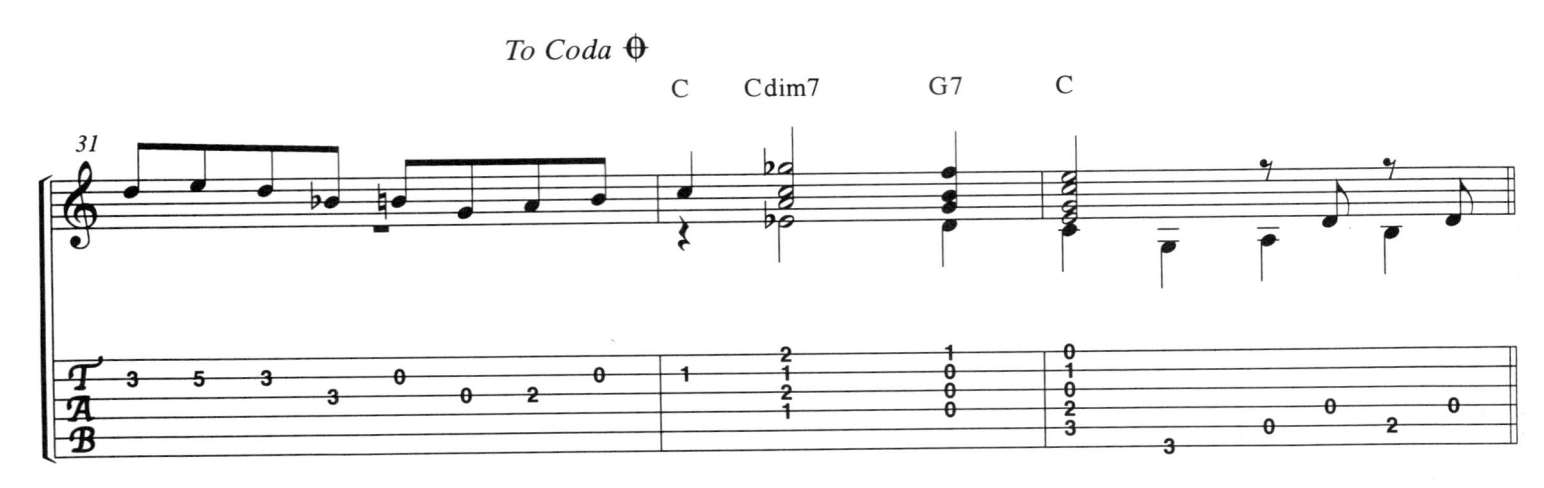

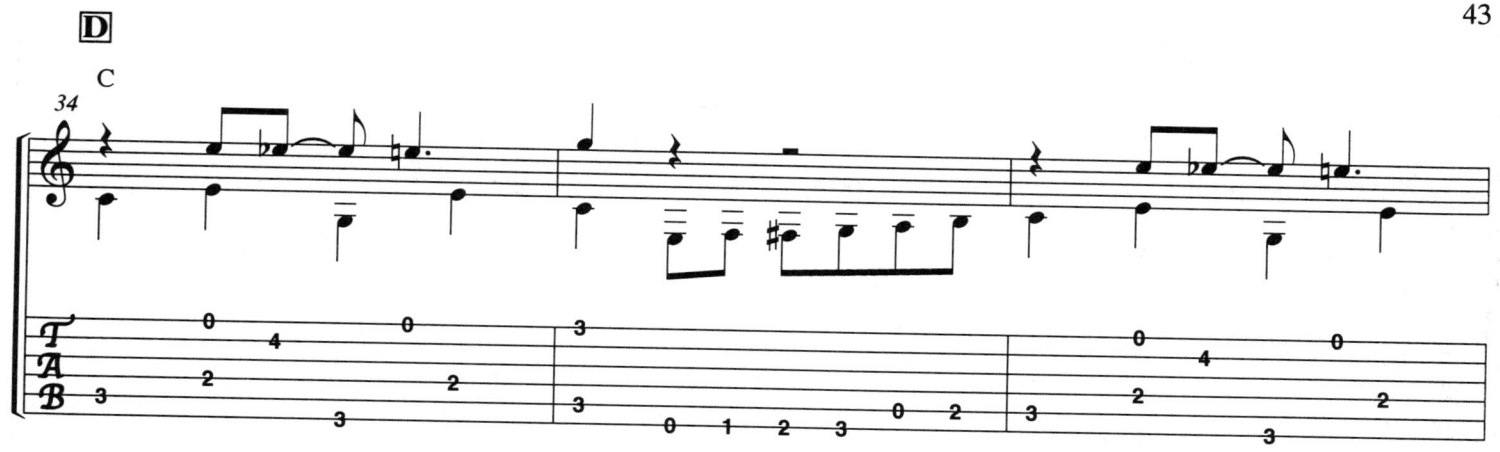

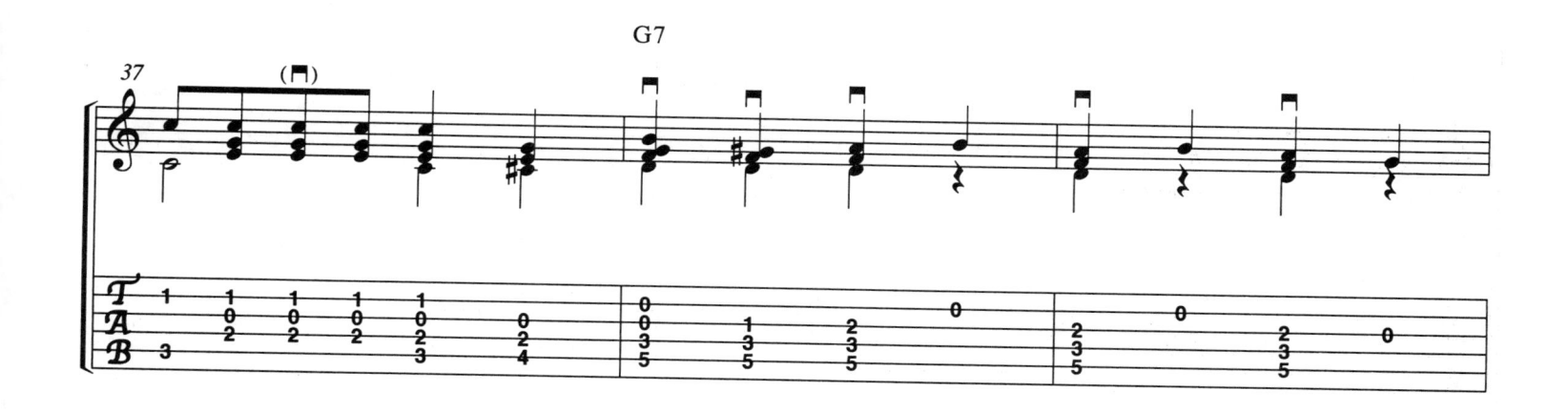

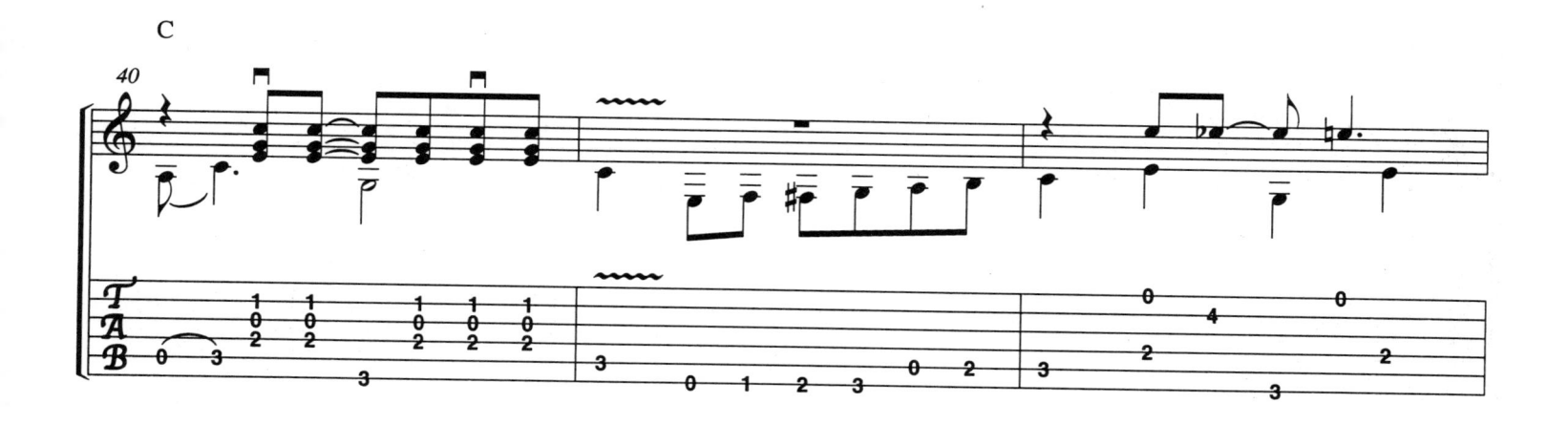

Fishin' in the Wind - 6 - 4
SAIR007

44

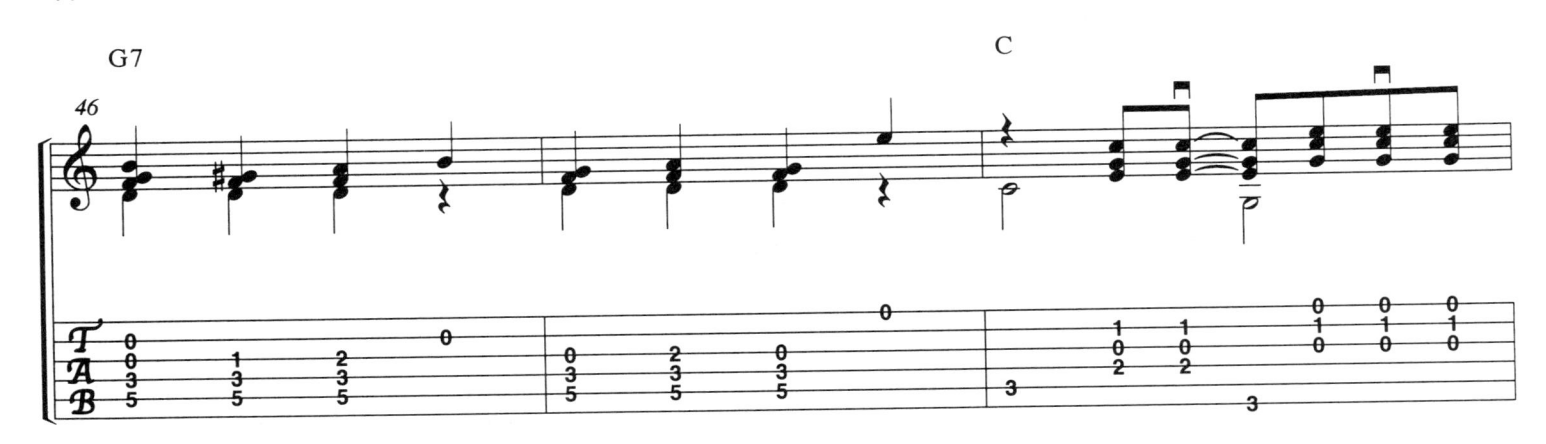

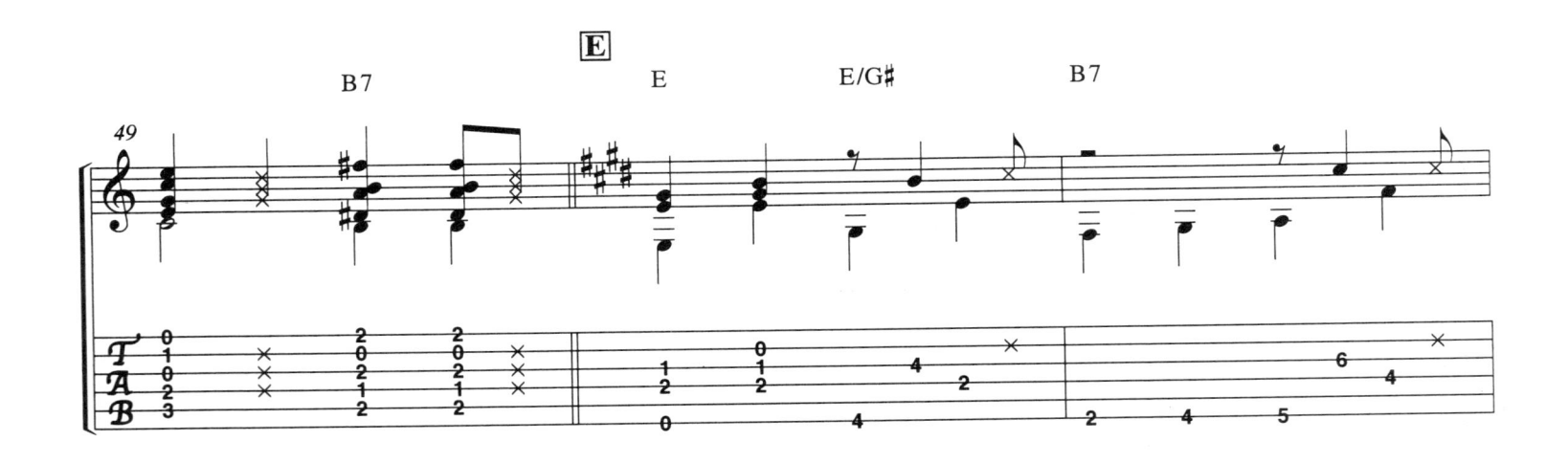

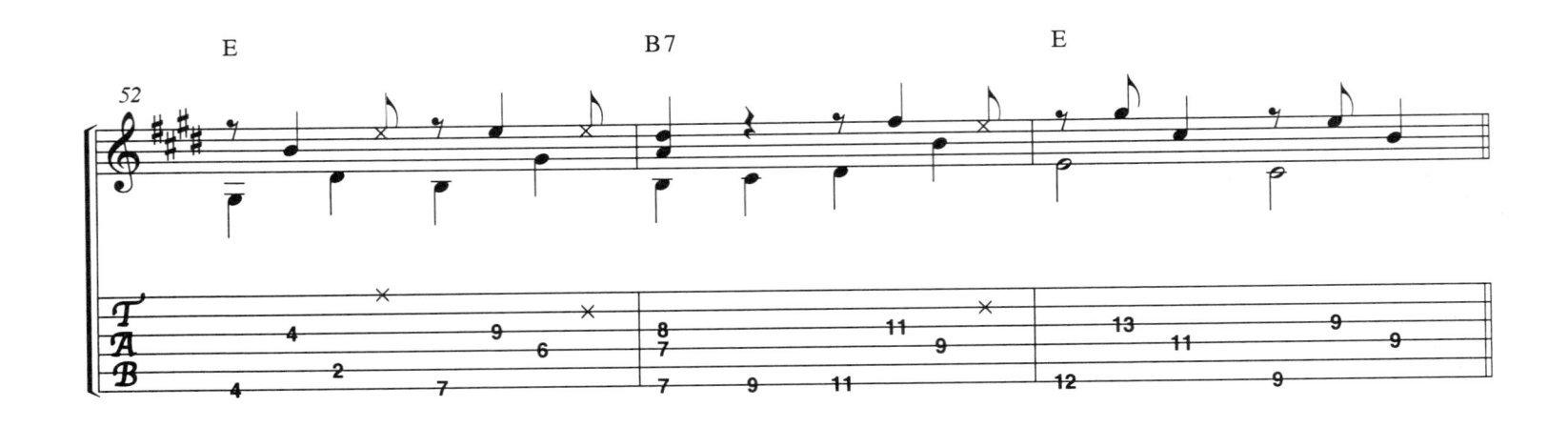

Fishin' in the Wind - 6 - 5
SAIR007

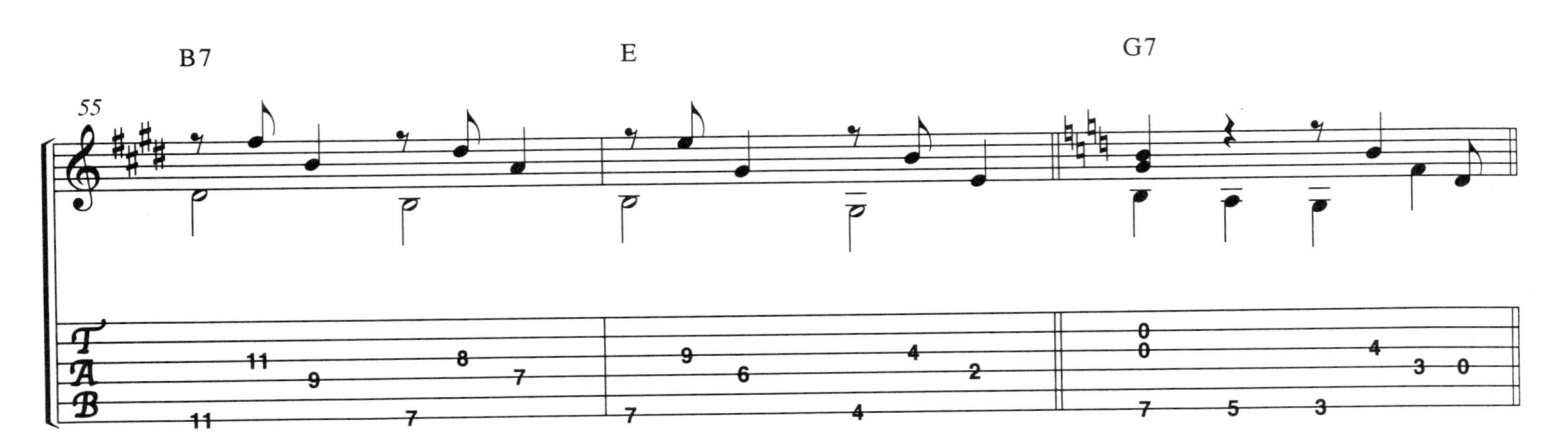

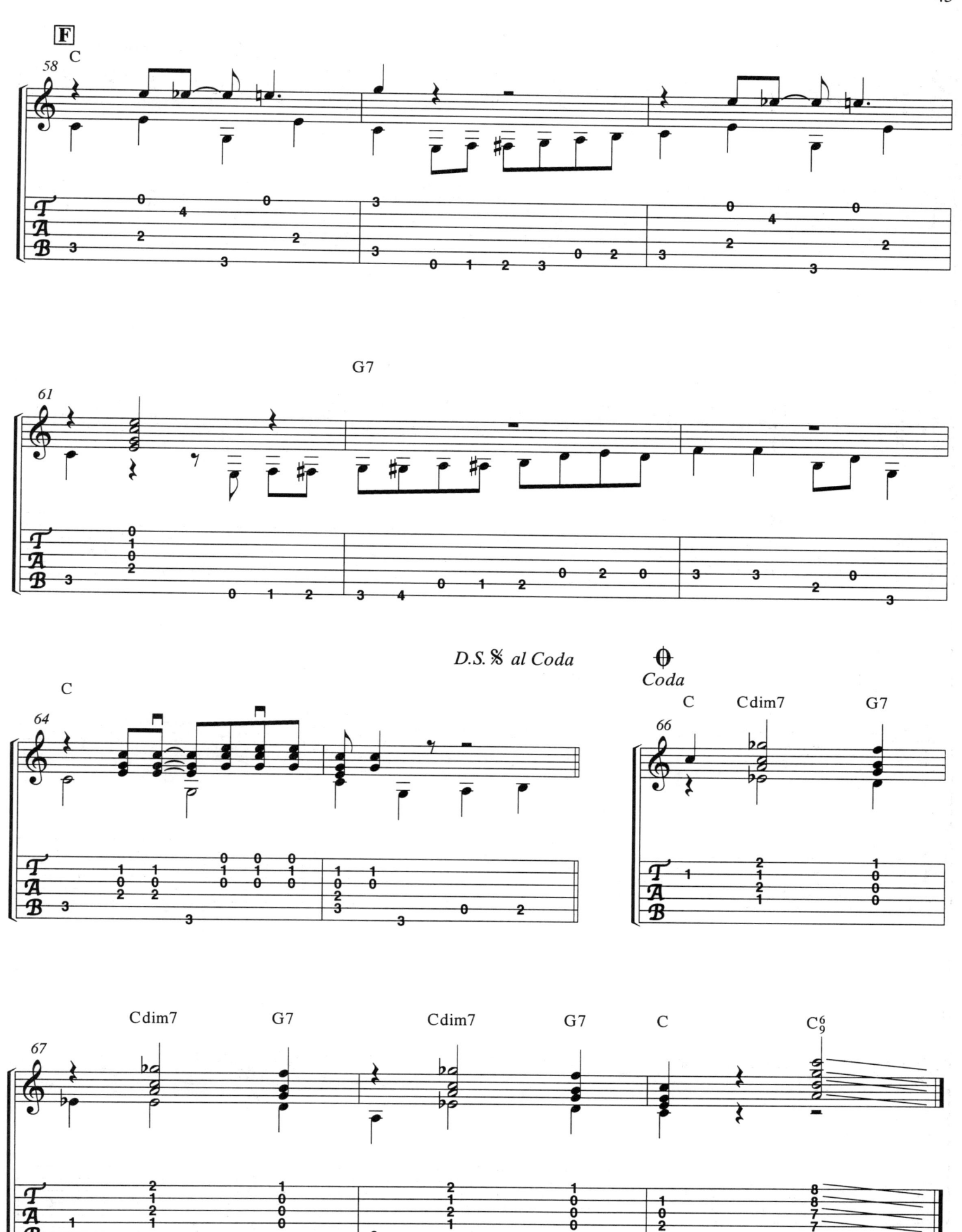

Fishin' in the Wind - 6 - 6
SAIR007

Jan's Song

By MIKE DOWLING

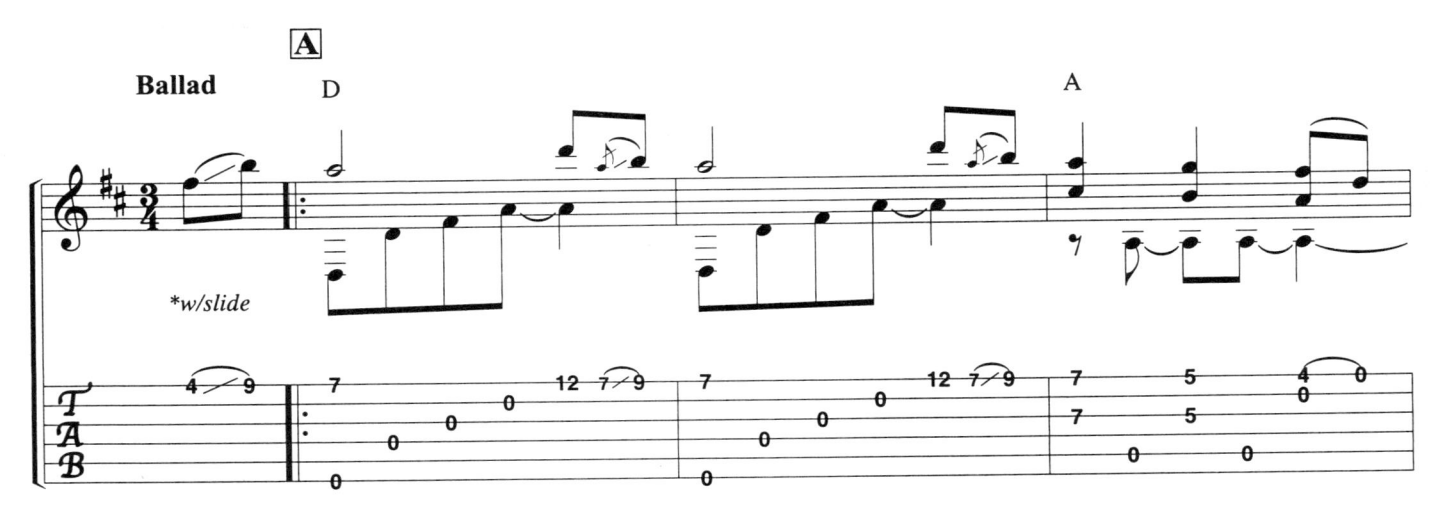

Open D tuning:
⑥ = D   ③ = F#
⑤ = A   ② = A
④ = D   ① = D

Ballad

*w/slide

*All fretted notes played w/slide unless otherwise indicated.

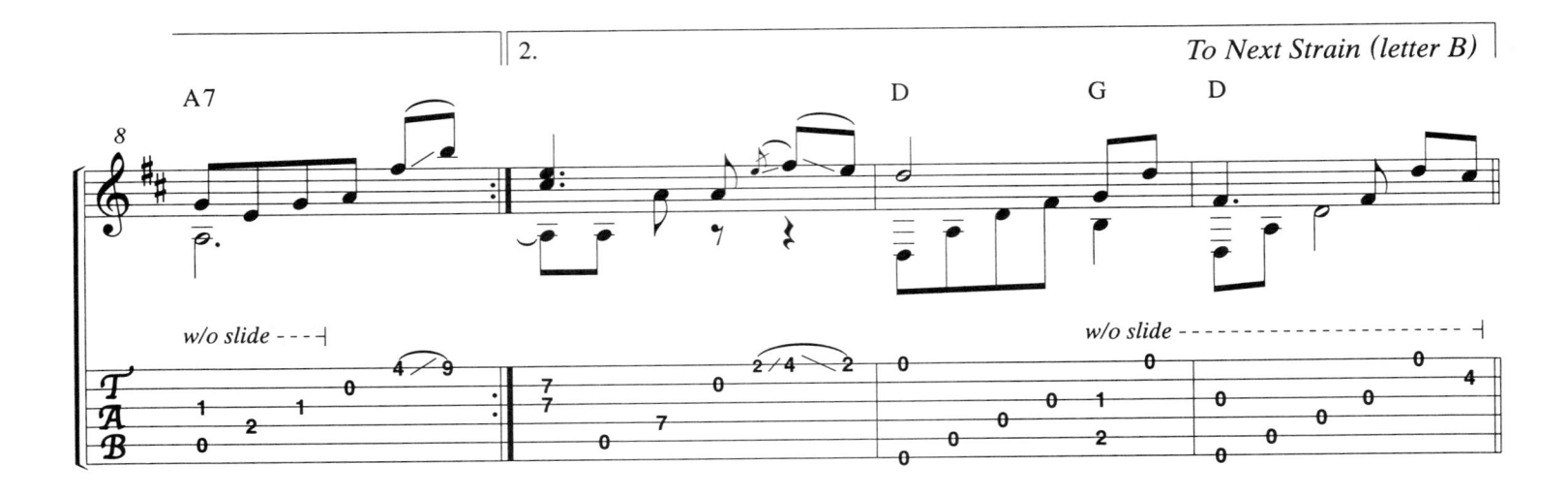

3.
To letter C
B
Bm
12
D
G
D
w/o slide
w/o slide
D/A
16
G
A
D
Bm
(w/o slide)
w/o slide
To Coda
E7
20
A7
(w/o slide)
C
D
23
A
3

27
1.
D
A7
no slide
T
A
B
31
2.
D.S. 𝄋 al Coda
D
G
D
w/o slide
Coda
34
D
A
38
A
D
D7/C
G/B
Gm6
w/o slide
42
D
E7
A7
D

Johnson City Rag

By MIKE DOWLING

Standard tuning

Brisk tempo

To Coda
D6/F♯ Dm6/F A/E A/C♯ F♯7 B9 E13 A
17
E7 A E7 A
21
A E7 A E7 B9 E7
25
1/4
A E7 A E7 A E7/B A7/C♯ D Dmaj7 D6 D
29
T
A
B

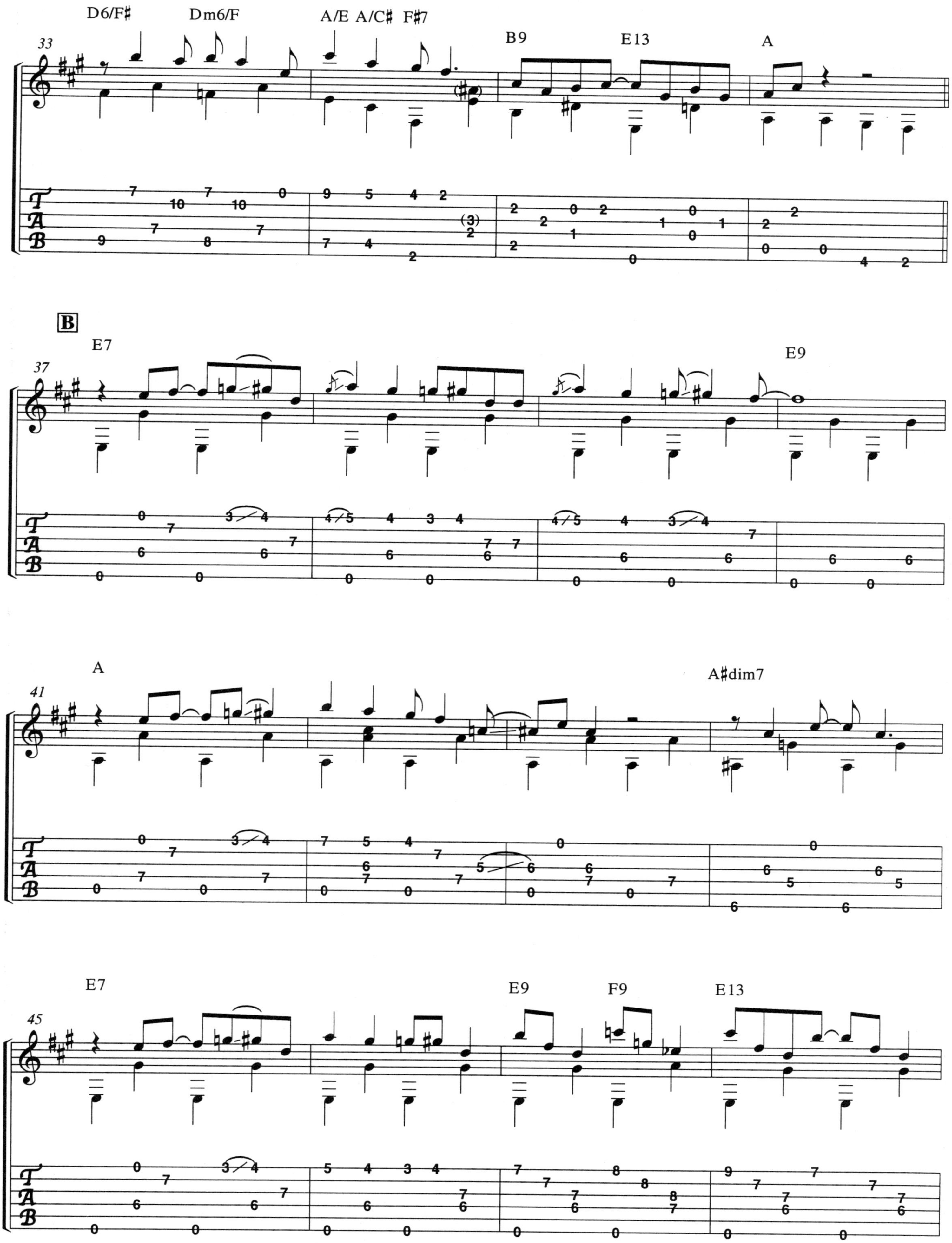
D6/F♯
Dm6/F
A/E A/C♯ F♯7
B9
E13
A
33
B
E7
E9
37
A
A♯dim7
41
E7
E9
F9
E13
45

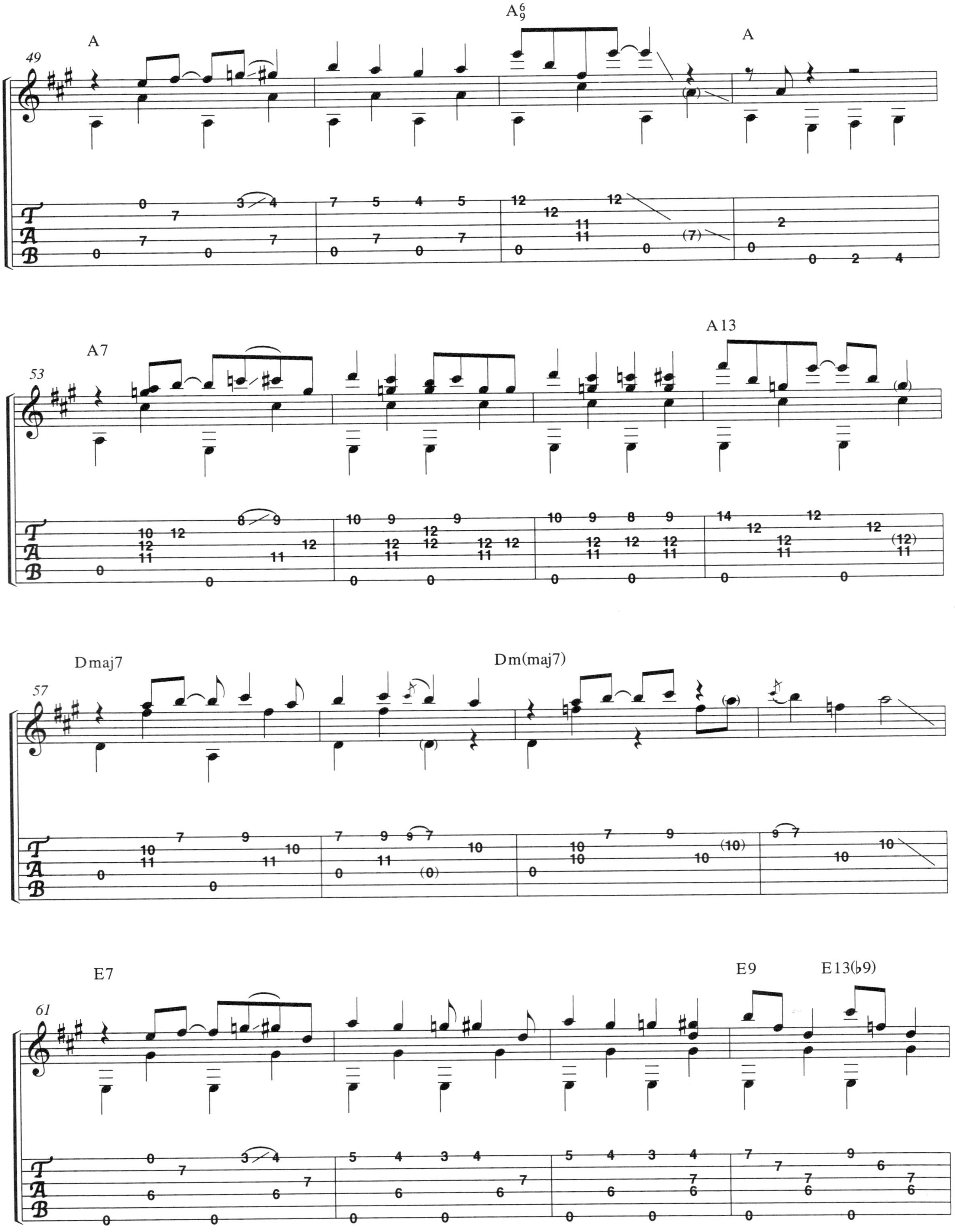
49
A
A6/9
A
53
A7
A13
57
Dmaj7
Dm(maj7)
61
E7
E9
E13(♭9)

65
A
F
E7
A1
69
A
E7
A
Adim7 E7
A
73
E7
A
B Bdim7 F♯7 B7
E7 E7(♭13)/B♭
77
A
E7
A
E7
A E7/B A7/C♯
D Dmaj7 D6 D

D6/F♯
Dm6/F
A/E A/C♯ F♯7
B9
E13
A
A7(♭9)
81
B1
E7
A
85
E7
Adim
A
89
E7
F7
A7
A13
93

D.S. 𝄋 al Coda
97
D6/F♯
Dm6/F
A/E A/C♯ F♯7
B9
E13
A
Coda
101
A
D6/F♯
Dm6/F
A
F♯9
104
B9
E13
A
N.C. (A)
(Adim7)
107
(A)
(F♯7)
(B7)
(E7)
A
A6/9

Minor Thing

By MIKE DOWLING and RANDY SABIEN

Standard tuning

*Roll with p, i, m, a.

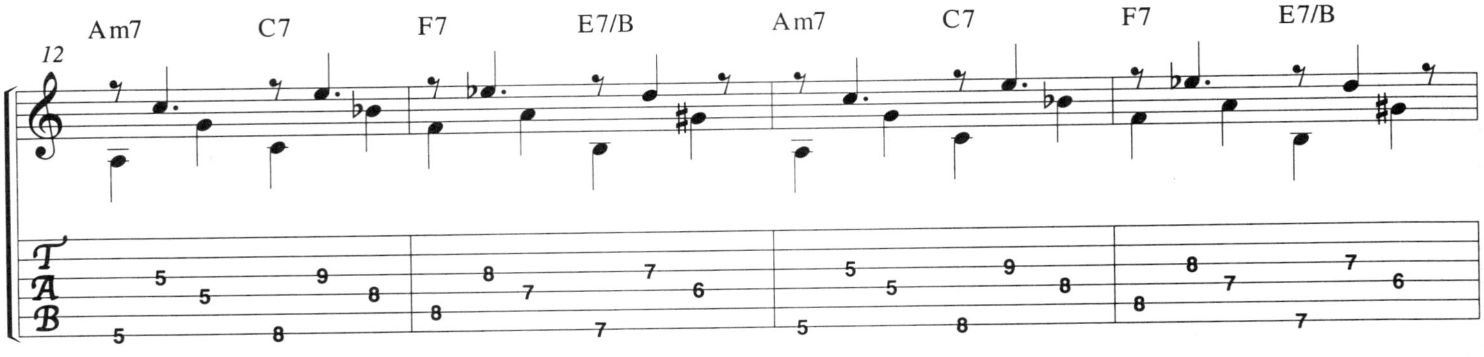

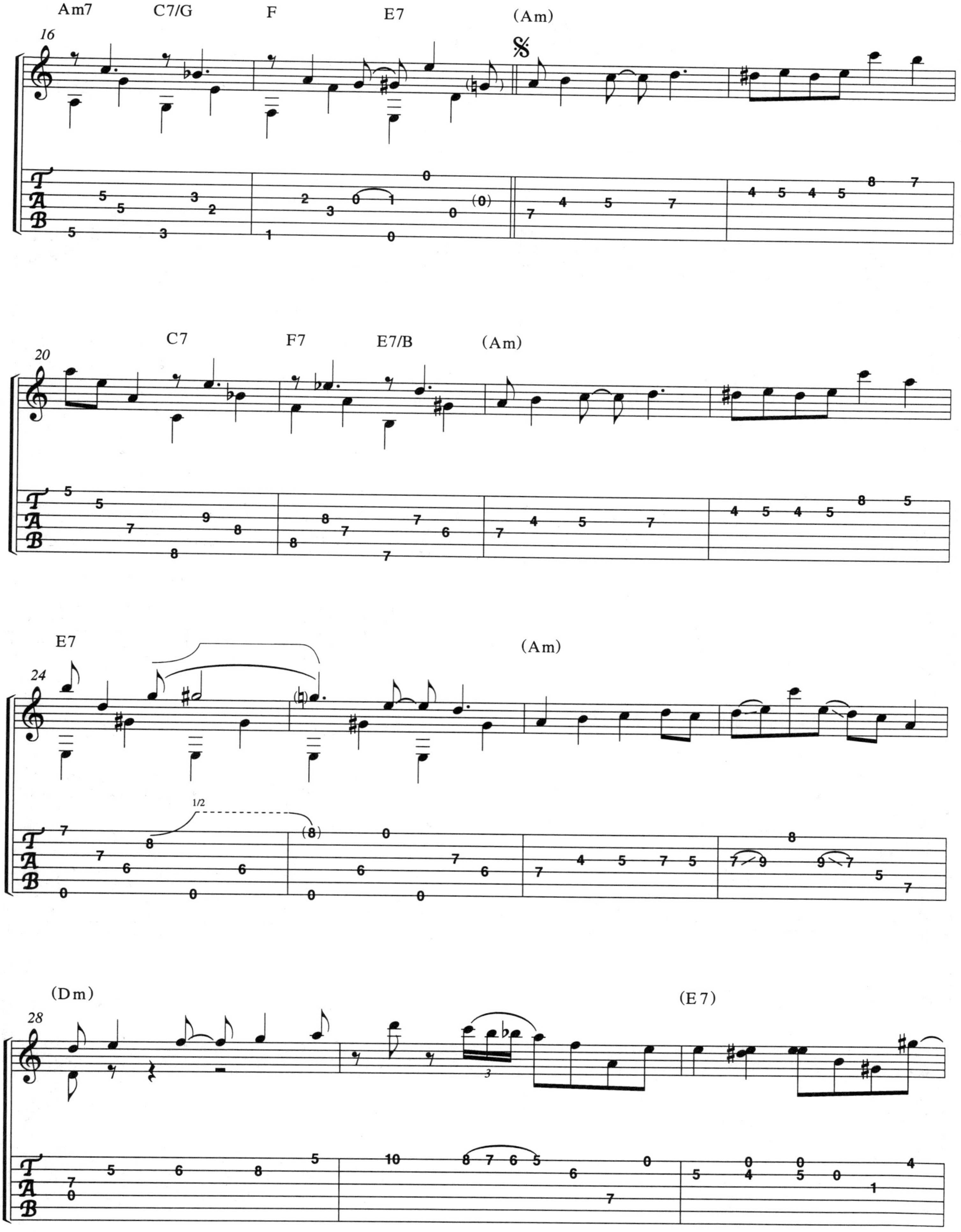
Am7
C7/G
F
E7
(Am)
C7
F7
E7/B
(Am)
E7
(Am)
(Dm)
(E7)

E7(♭13 ♭9)
To Coda
Am7
31
Dm7
34
Am7
Dm7
38
Ddim7
Am7
A7
Dm7
42
Am7
E7
Am7
TAB

59

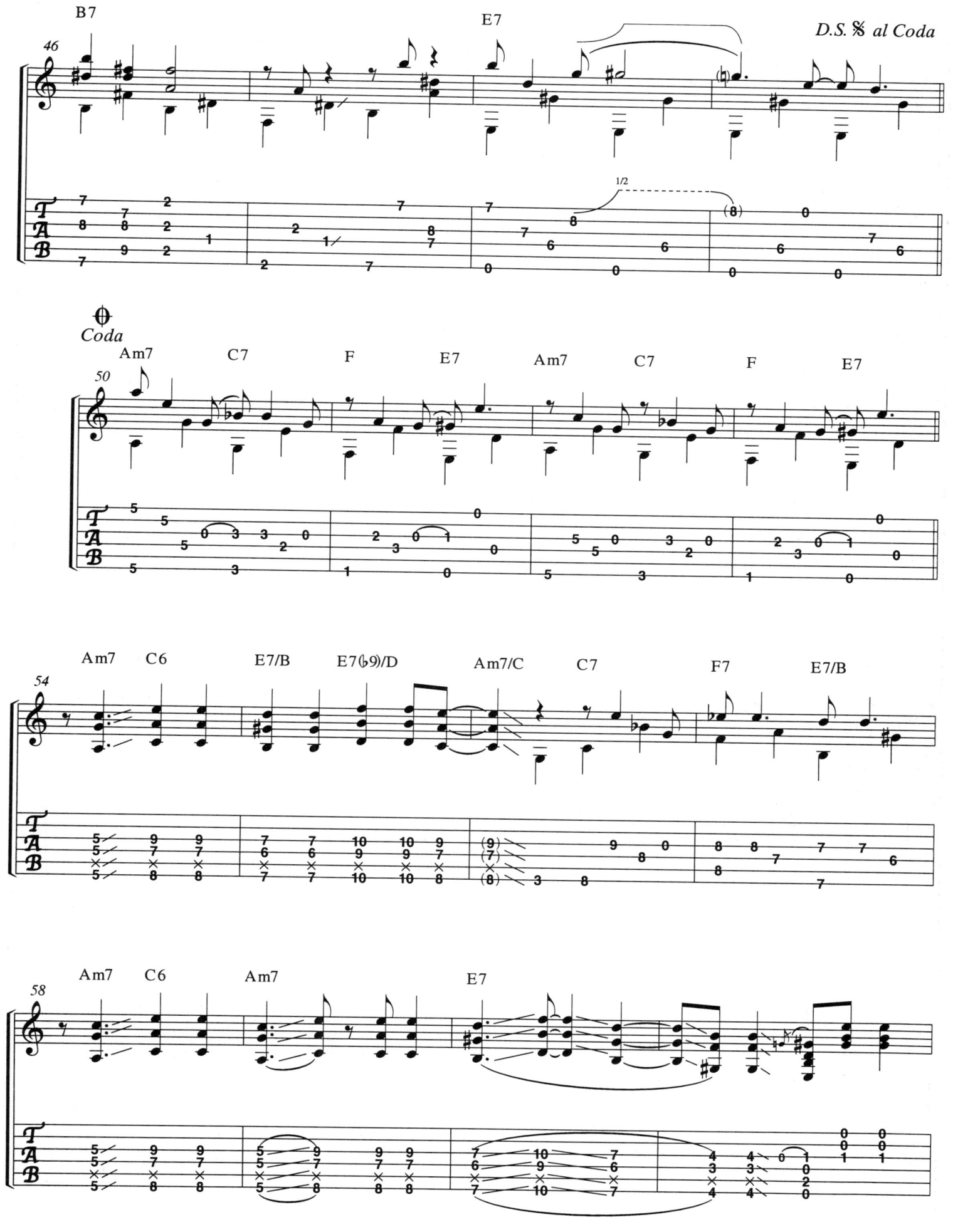

62
Am7
E7/B
Am7/C
Dm7
A7(♭9)/E
Dm7
66
E7(♯9)
E7
E7(♯9)
Am
F7/C
E7/B
Am
70
Dm7
Am7
74
(Dm)
(Am)
A7
Dm7
78
Am7
B7

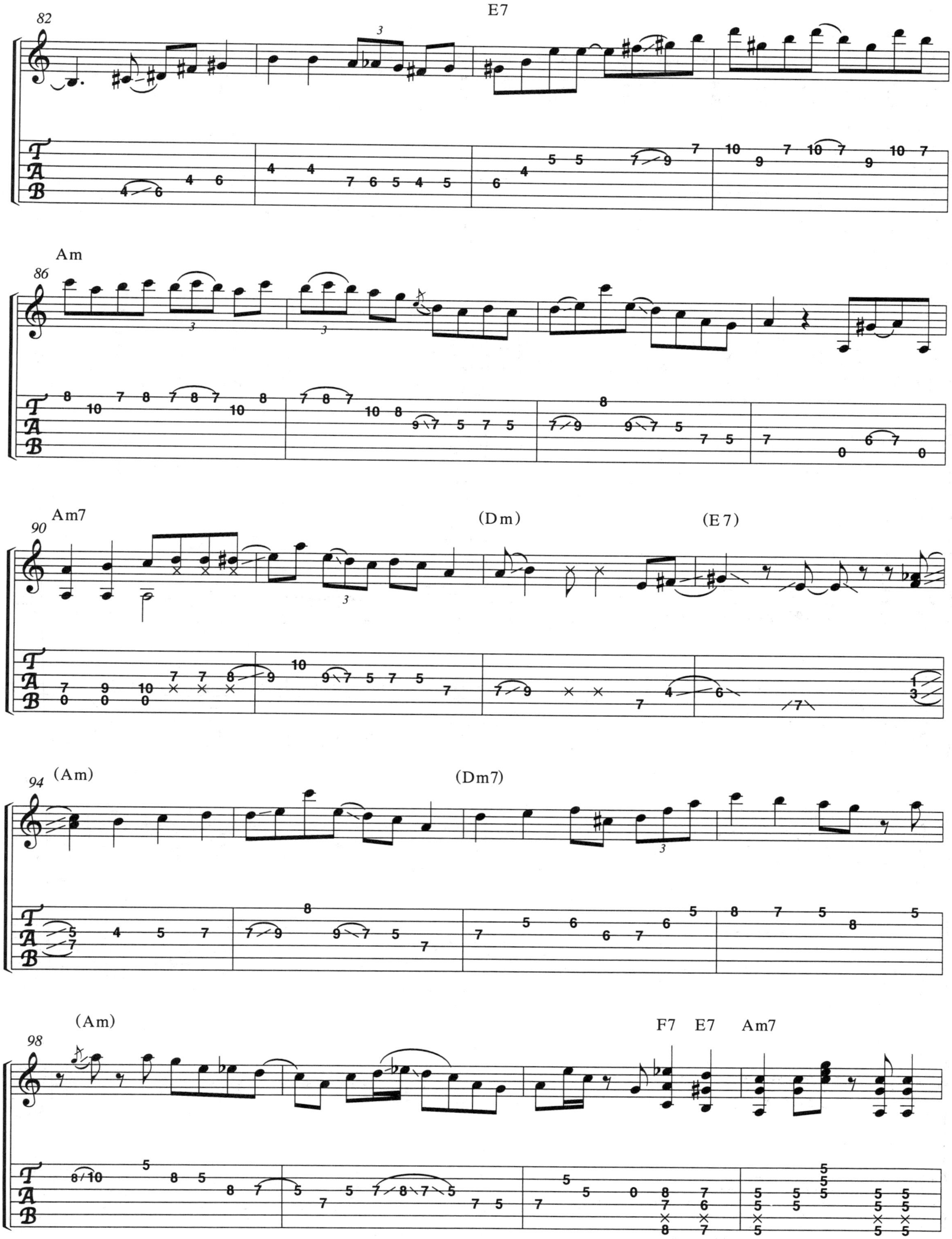
82
E7
86
Am
90
Am7
(Dm)
(E7)
94
(Am)
(Dm7)
98
(Am)
F7
E7
Am7

Dm7
Am7
102
Dm7
E7
Am7
Am6
A7
A7
106
Dm7
Dm7
Am
Dm6
Am
110
B7
E9
114

(Am)
(Dm)
118
1/4
1/4
(Am)
122
(E7)
(Am)
126
(Dm)
(Am)
E7(♭13 ♭9)
E7(♭9)
Am7
F7
E7
Am7
E7
130
(Am)
C7/G
F
E7
134

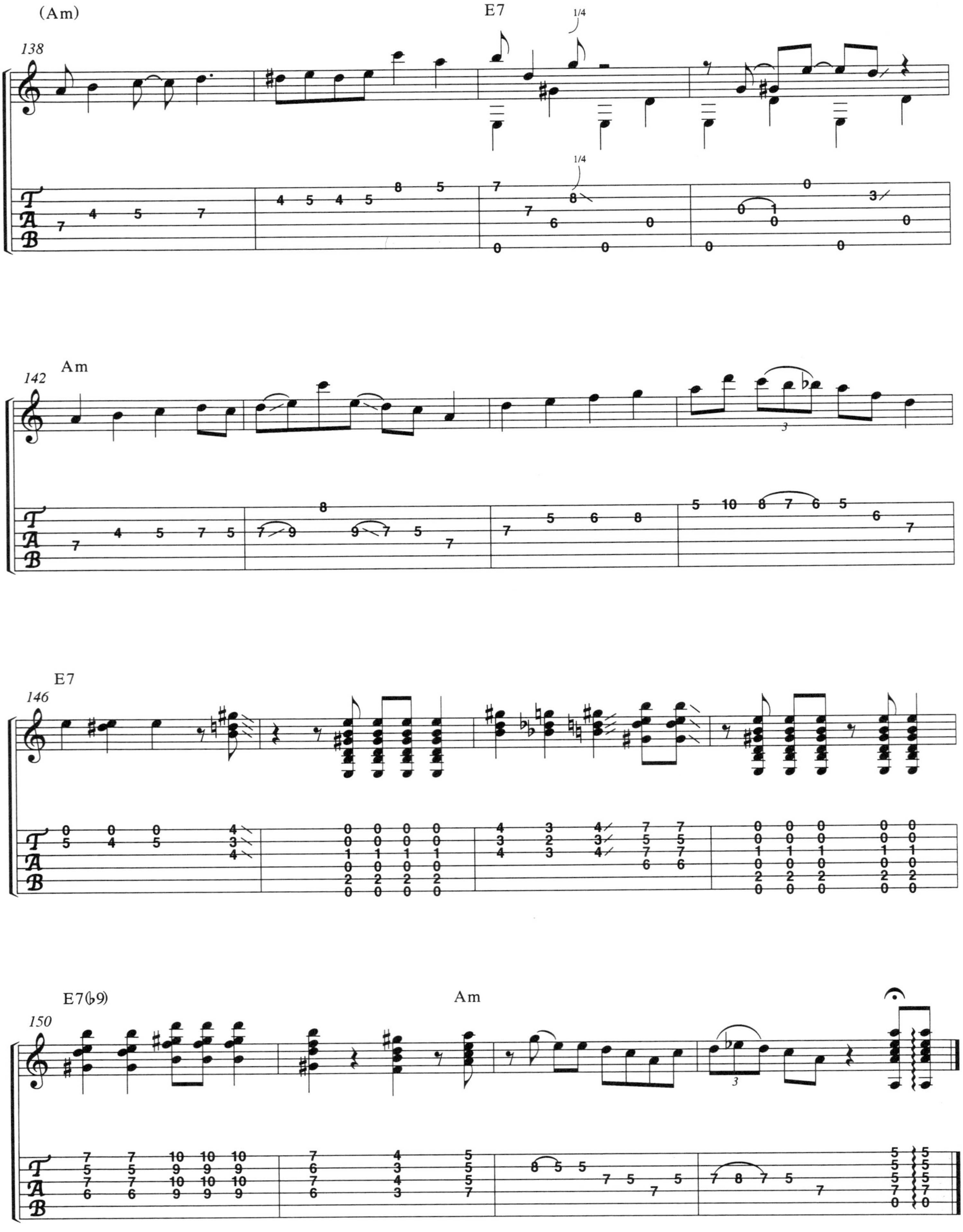
(Am)
E7
1/4
138
1/4
Am
142
E7
146
E7(♭9)
Am
150

Nitpickin'

By MIKE DOWLING

Standard tuning

Allegro

16
B7(♯5)
E9(♯5)
A7(♯5)
D13
2.
A9
Am7
20
D13
D13(♭9)
G7
B
C
24
G7(♭13)
C
G7
28
G9 (♭13)
C
32
G7(♭13)
C
Em7
A7

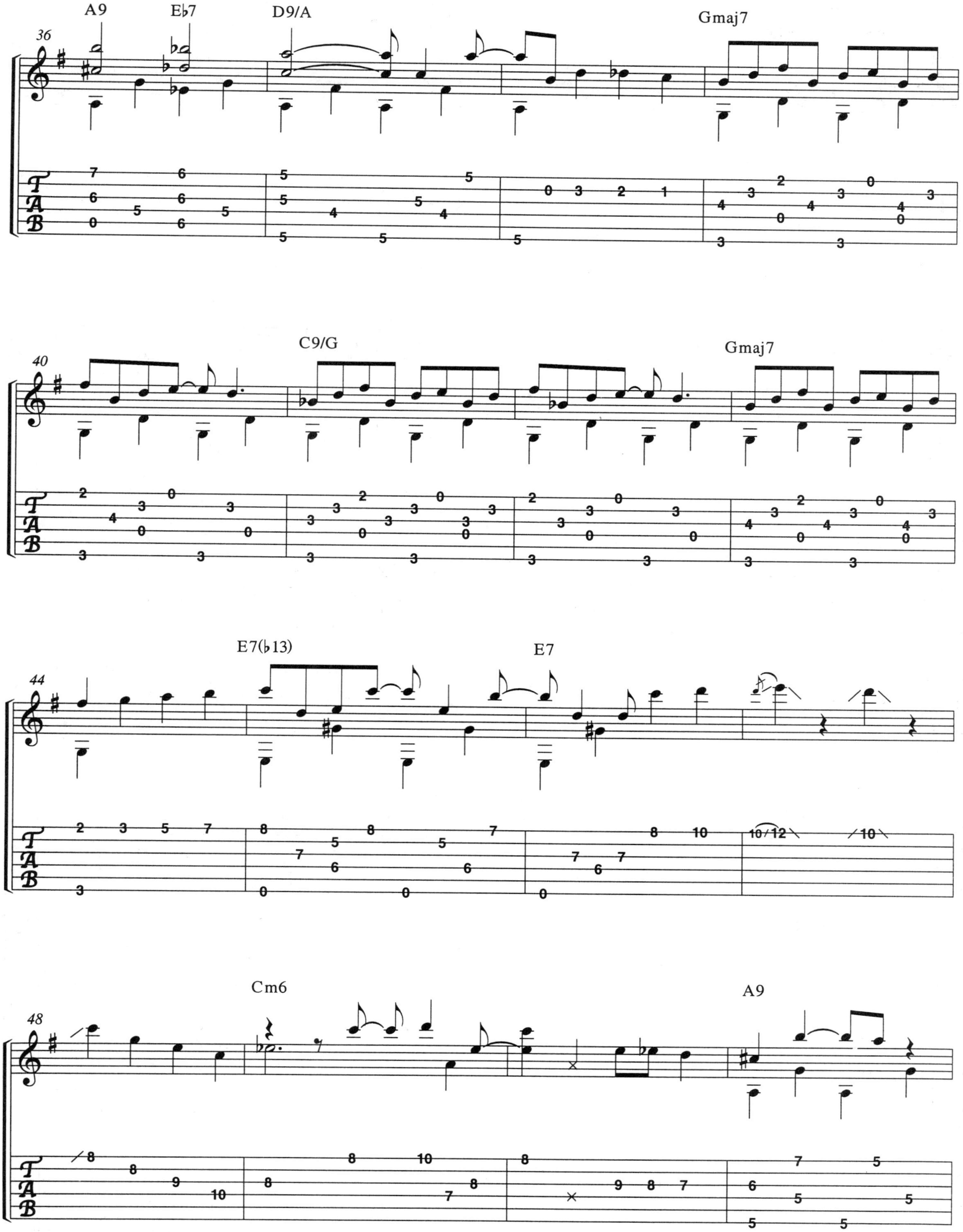

36
A9
E♭7
D9/A
Gmaj7
40
C9/G
Gmaj7
44
E7(♭13)
E7
48
Cm6
A9
T
A
B

Nitpickin' - 7 - 4

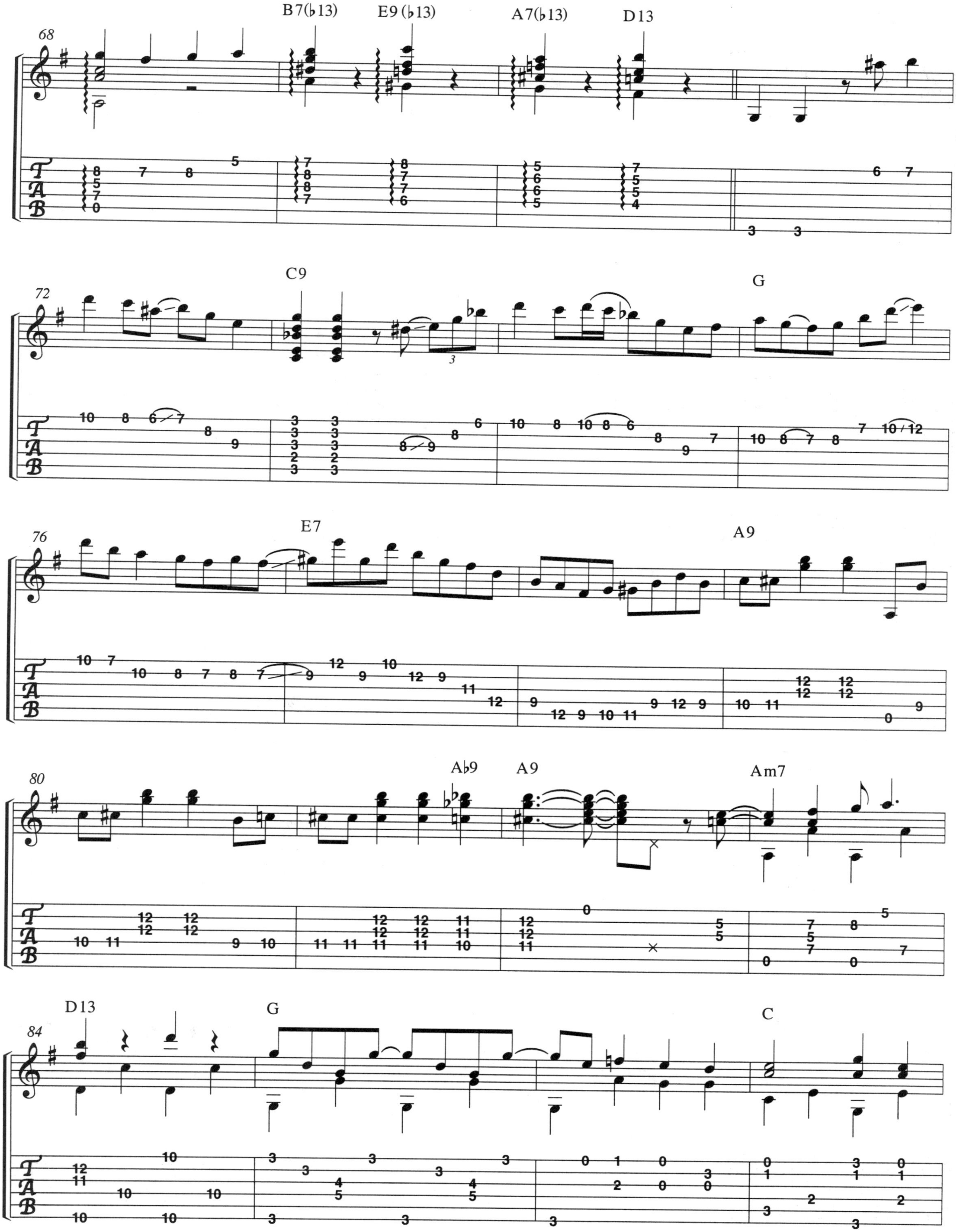
68
B7(♭13)
E9(♭13)
A7(♭13)
D13
T
A
B
72
C9
G
76
E7
A9
80
A♭9
A9
Am7
84
D13
G
C

88
G7(♭13)
C
G7
92
G
G7(♭13)
C
C
96
G7(♭13)
C
Em
A7
100
A9
E♭7
D7
C♯7
D7
Gmaj7
104
C9/G
Gmaj7

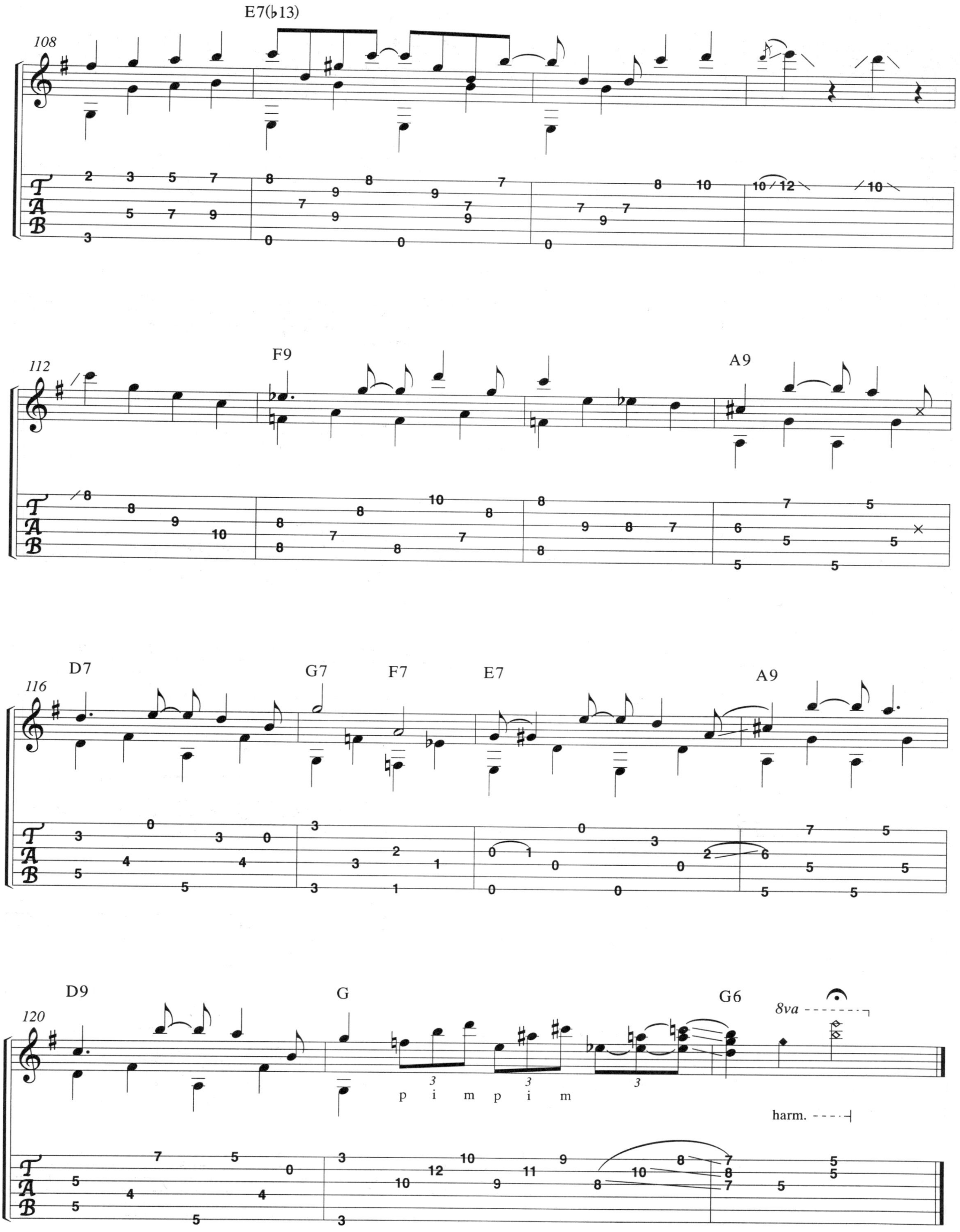
108
E7(♭13)
112
F9
A9
116
D7
G7
F7
E7
A9
120
D9
G
G6
8va
p i m p i m
harm.

Rocky Road

Traditional
Arranged by MIKE DOWLING and BRUCE NEMEROV

Open D tuning:
⑥ = D ③ = F#
⑤ = A ② = A
④ = D ① = D

© 2001 TableTop Music (ASCAP) and Solid Air Music (ASCAP)
All Rights Reserved

*Brush with back of right-hand fingernails to produce a percussive backbeat.

Rocky Road - 5 - 2
SAIR007

*Hit strings while muting w/right palm.

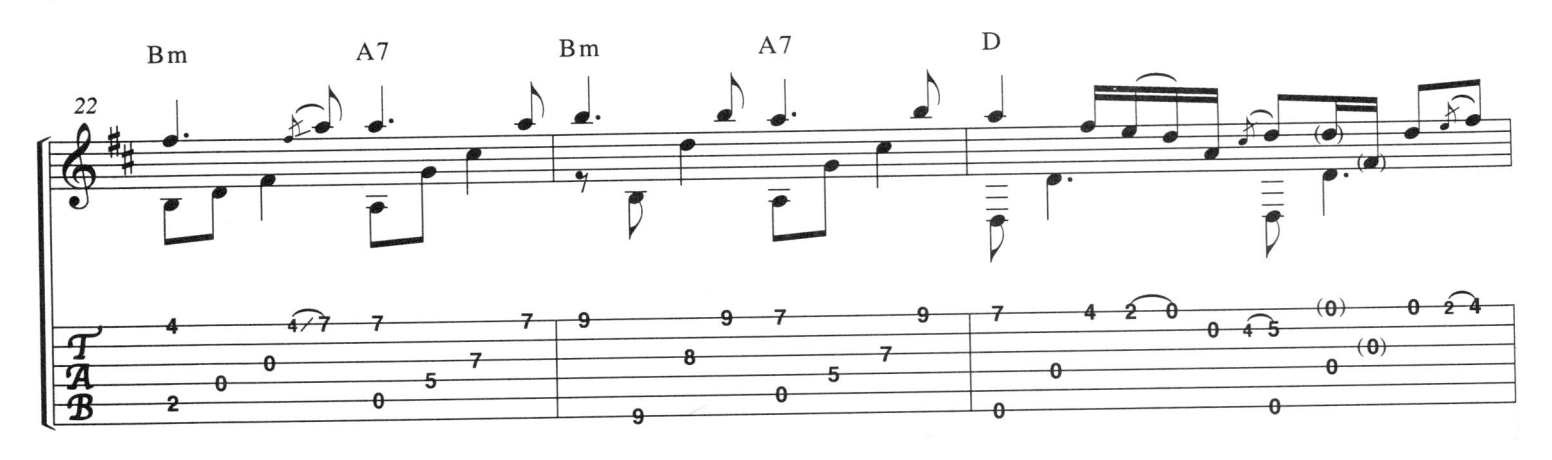

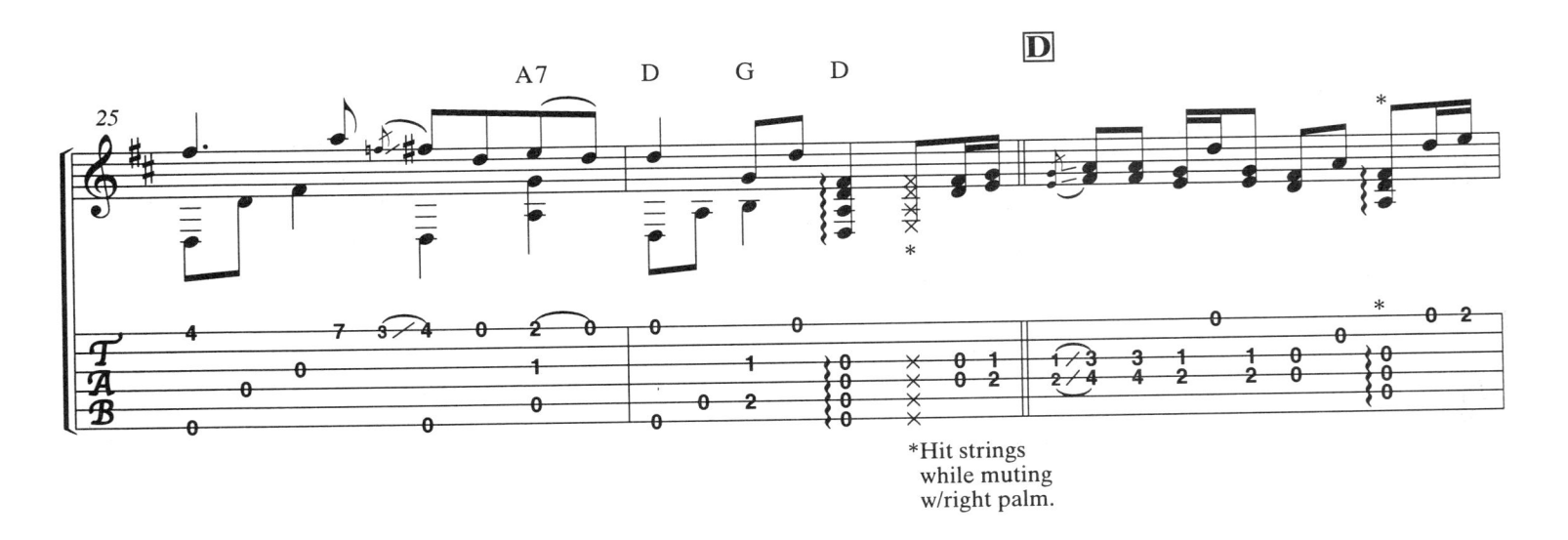

Rocky Road - 5 - 3

75

Rocky Road - 5 - 5

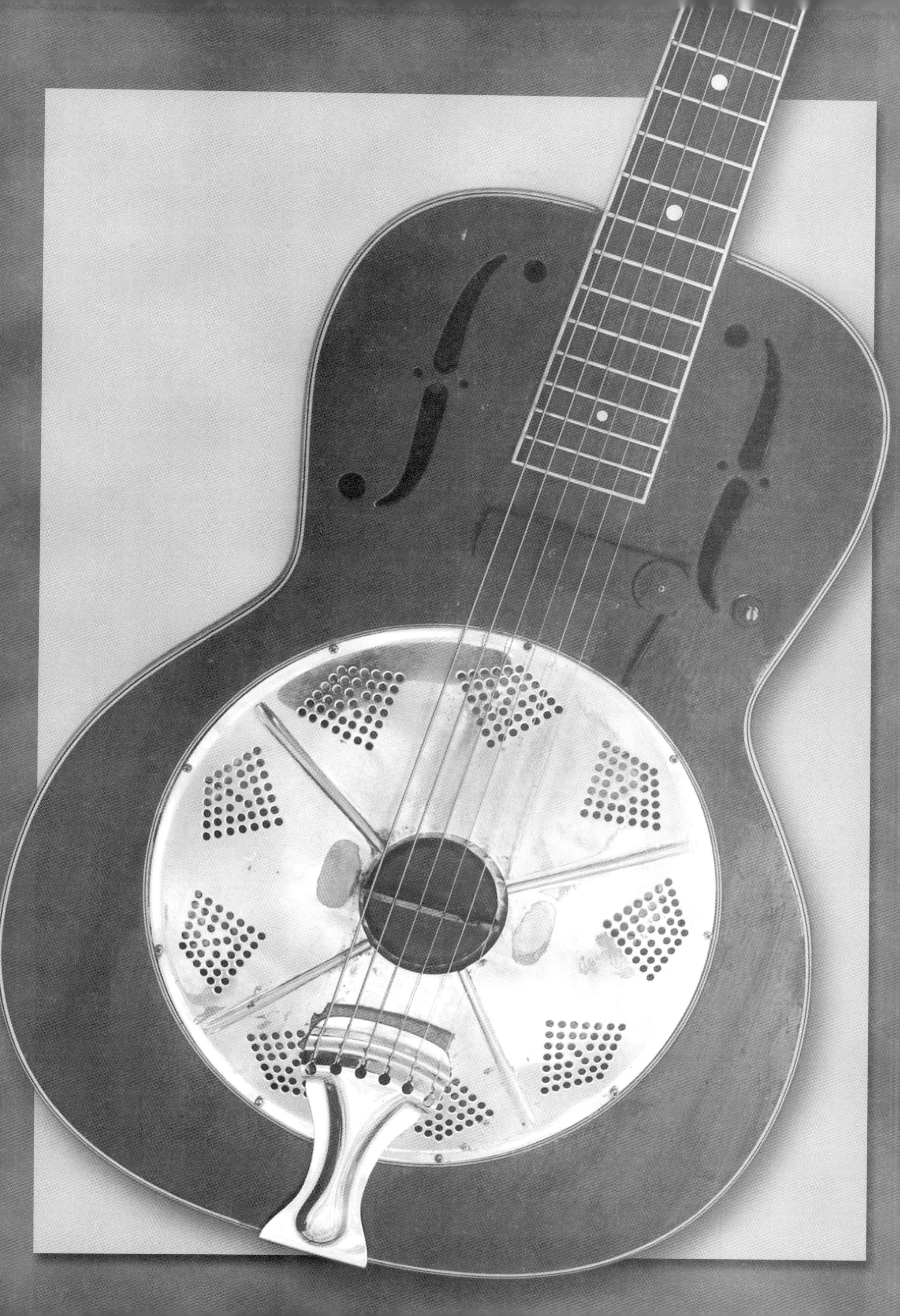

Rosalie

Traditional
Arranged by MIKE DOWLING

Open G tuning:
⑥ = D ③ = G
⑤ = G ② = B
④ = D ① = D

A

Moderately ♩ = 80

mf
fingerstyle

Cont. backbeat throughout

*Brush with back of right-hand fingernails to produce a percussive backbeat.

B

Rosalie - 6 - 1
SAIR007

© 1995 TableTop Music (ASCAP) and Solid Air Music (ASCAP)
All Rights Reserved

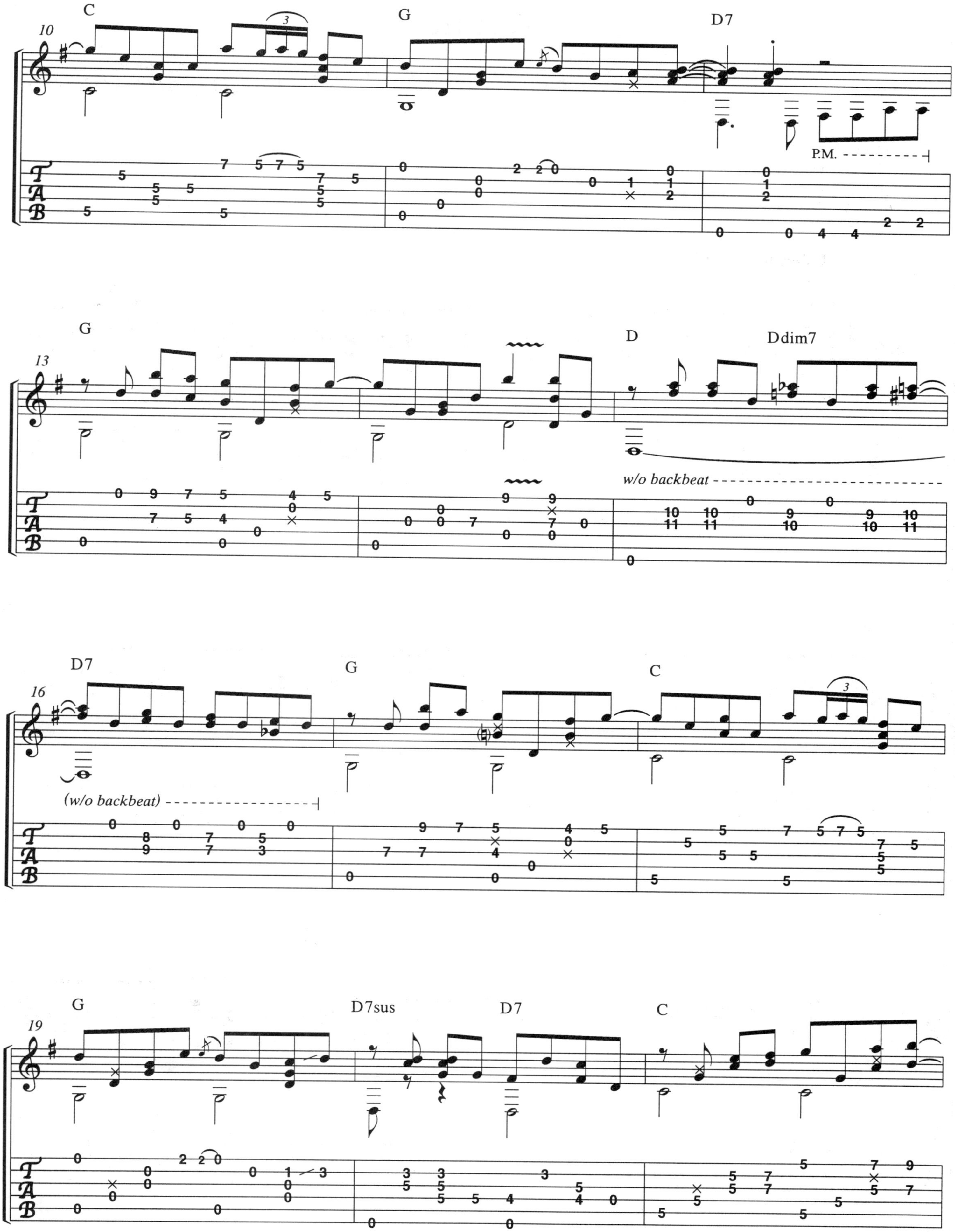
C
G
D7
P.M.
G
D
Ddim7
w/o backbeat
D7
G
C
(w/o backbeat)
G
D7sus
D7
C

22
G
D7
G
D
C
G
w/o backbeat
C
25
G
C
G
D7sus
D7
28
31
D
Ddim7
D7
G
w/o backbeat

C
G
D7sus
D7
C
G
D7
G
D
C
w/o backbeat
G
D
D
G
(w/o backbeat)
D
G
w/o backbeat

46
A7
D7
w/o backbeat
49
G
C
G
52
D7sus
D7
C
G
D7
55
G
D
C
G
To Coda
E
G
w/o backbeat

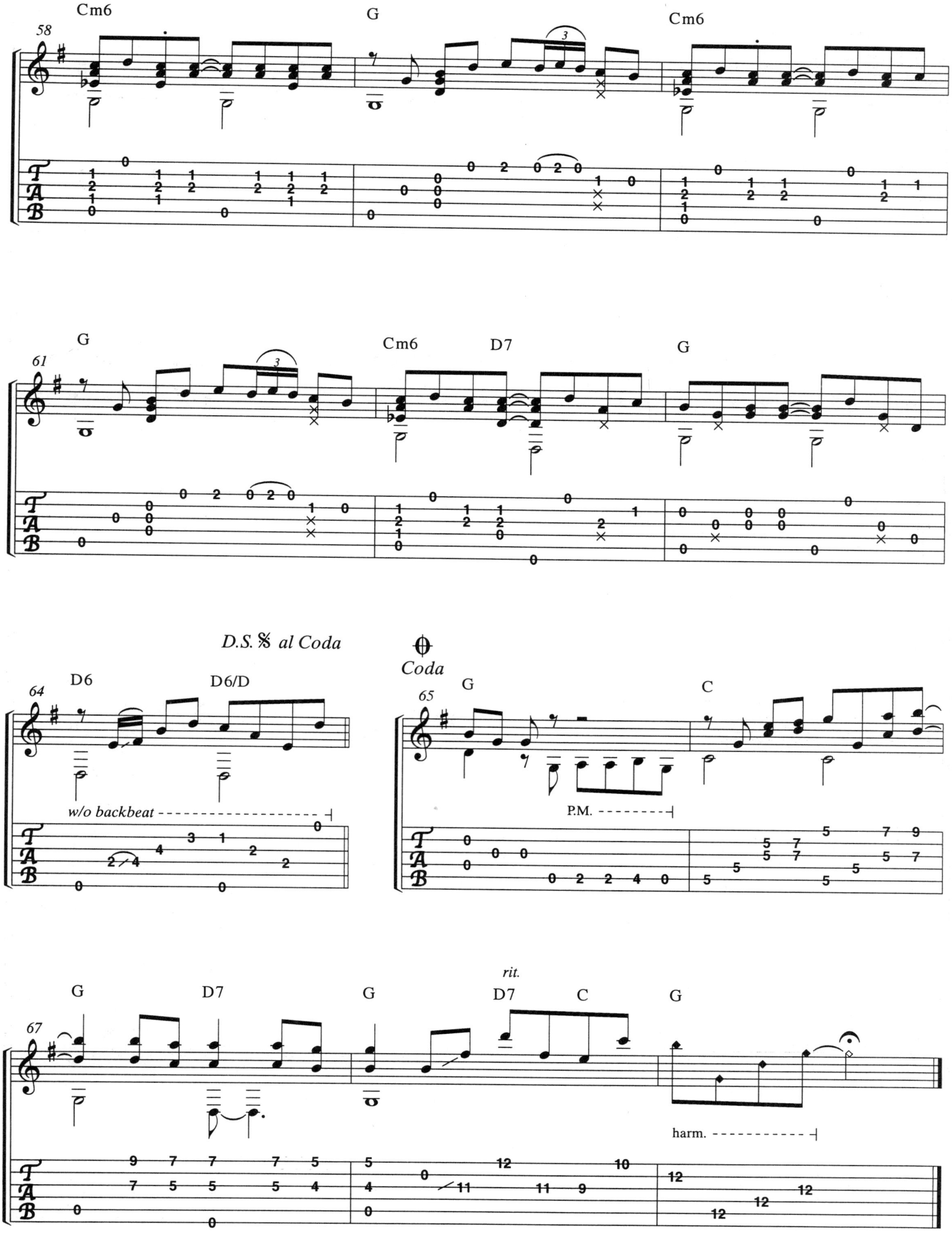
Cm6
G
Cm6
G
Cm6
D7
G
D.S. 𝄋 al Coda
Coda
D6
D6/D
w/o backbeat
G
C
P.M.
G
D7
G
rit.
D7
C
G
harm.

Shufflin'

By MIKE DOWLING

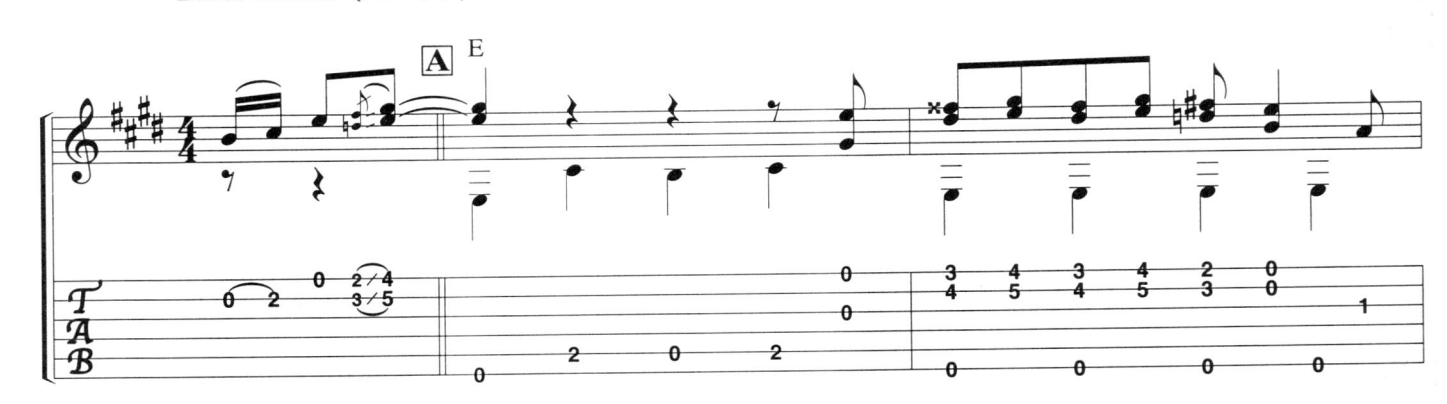

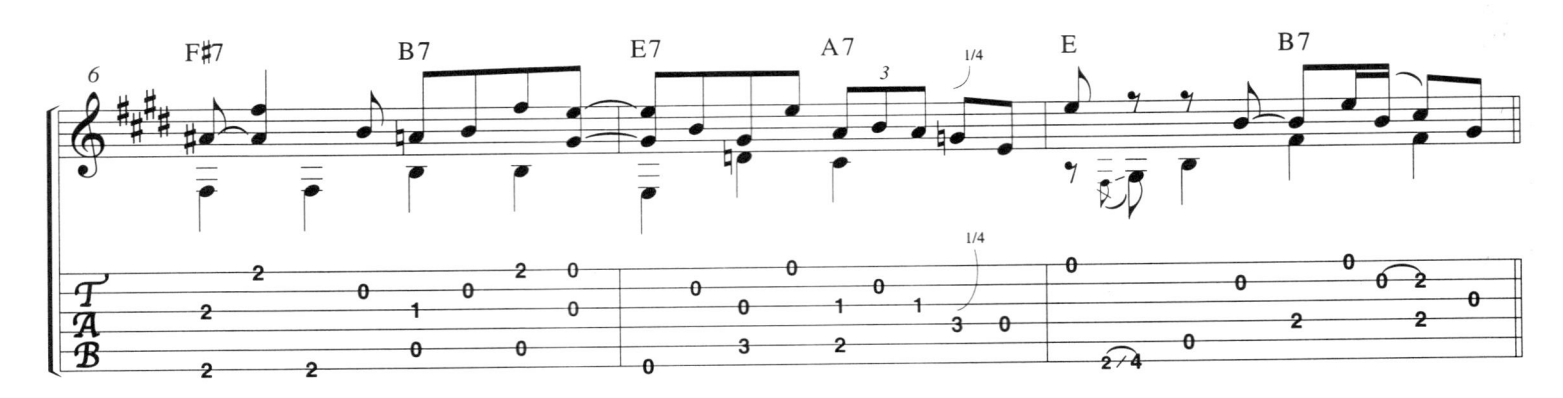

Open E tuning:
- ⑥ = E   ③ = G#
- ⑤ = B   ② = B
- ④ = E   ① = E

Blues shuffle ($\sqrt{}\sqrt{} = \sqrt{}^3\sqrt{}$)

Shufflin' - 6 - 1
SAIR007

© 2001 TableTop Music (ASCAP) and Solid Air Music (ASCAP)
All Rights Reserved

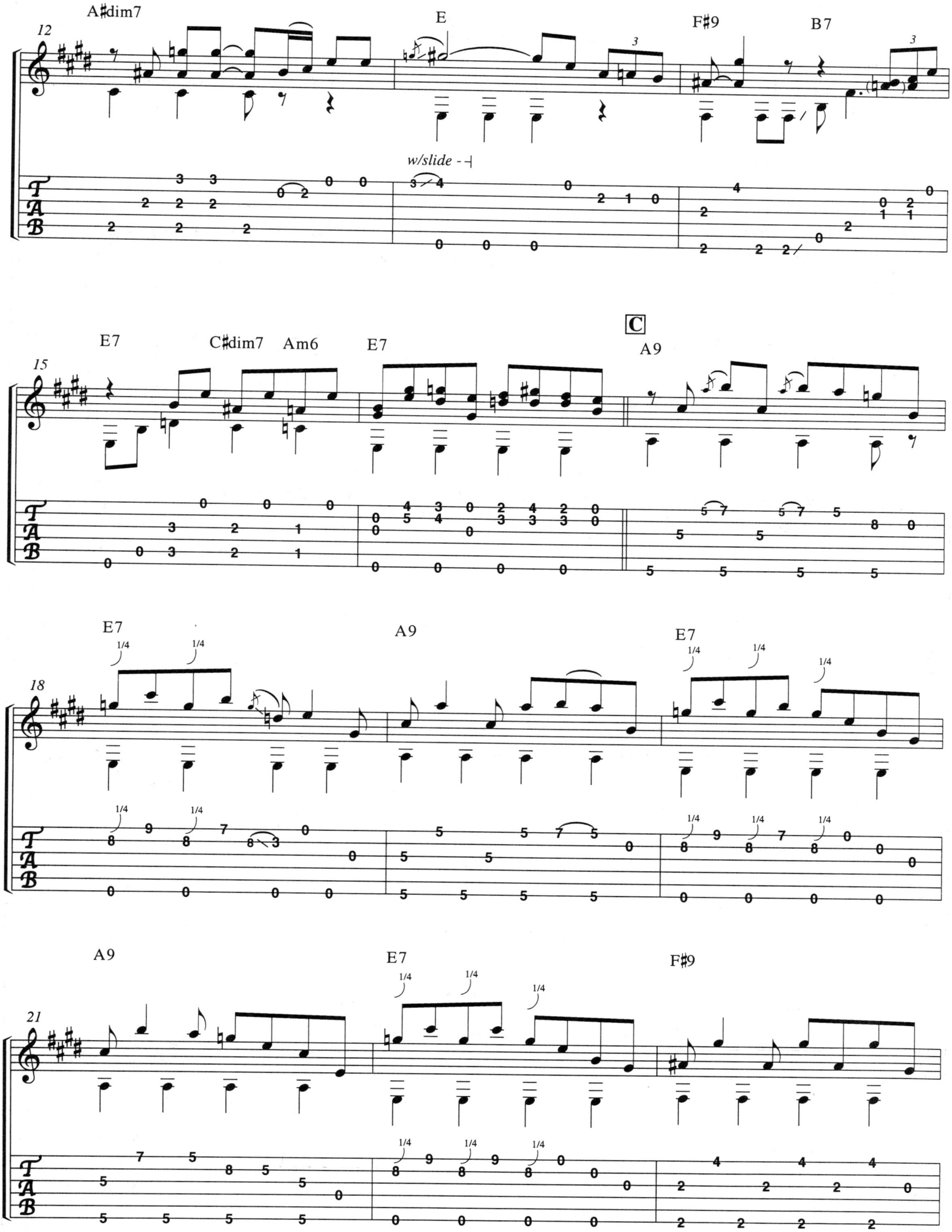
A♯dim7
E
F♯9
B7
w/slide
E7
C♯dim7
Am6
E7
C
A9
E7
A9
E7
A9
E7
F♯9

D
E
B7
24
w/slide
A7
A♯dim7
E
27
w/slide
F♯9
B7
E
E7
A
E
B7
30
1/4
E
E7
A9
33
1/4
let ring

36
E13
F♯7
B7
1/4
3
let ring
39
E
E7
C♯dim7
Cdim7
E
B7
F
straight 8 ths
w/slide
42
E7
A7
A♯dim7
w/slide
45
E
F♯7
B7
E
w/slide
T
A
B

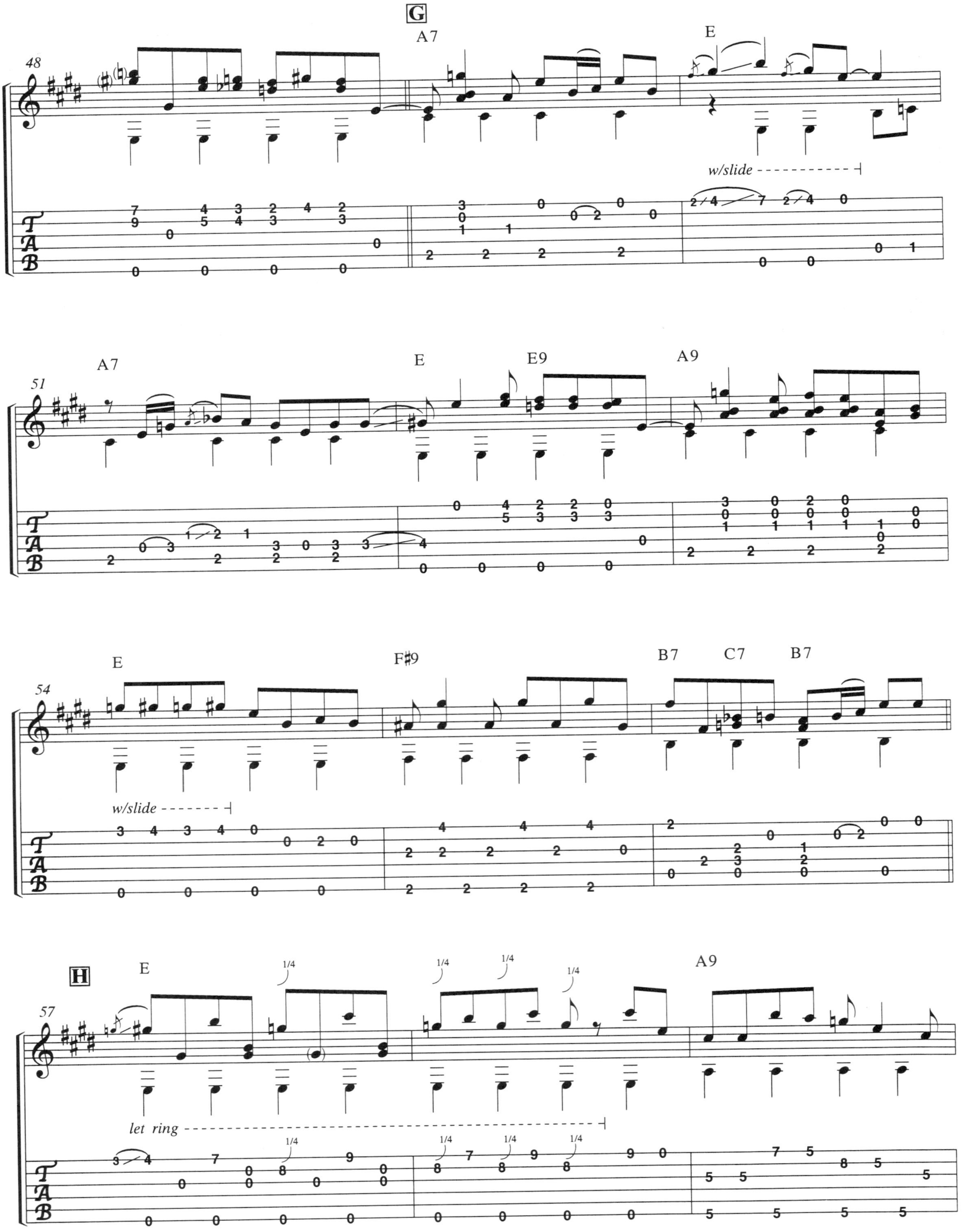
G
A7
E
w/slide
A7
E
E9
A9
E
F♯9
B7
C7
B7
w/slide
H
E
1/4
A9
let ring

Shufflin' - 6 - 6

Siboney

Spanish Lyrics and Music by
ERNESTO LECUONA
American Lyric by
DOLLY MORSE

Open G minor tuning:
⑥ = D   ③ = G
⑤ = G   ② = B♭
④ = D   ① = D

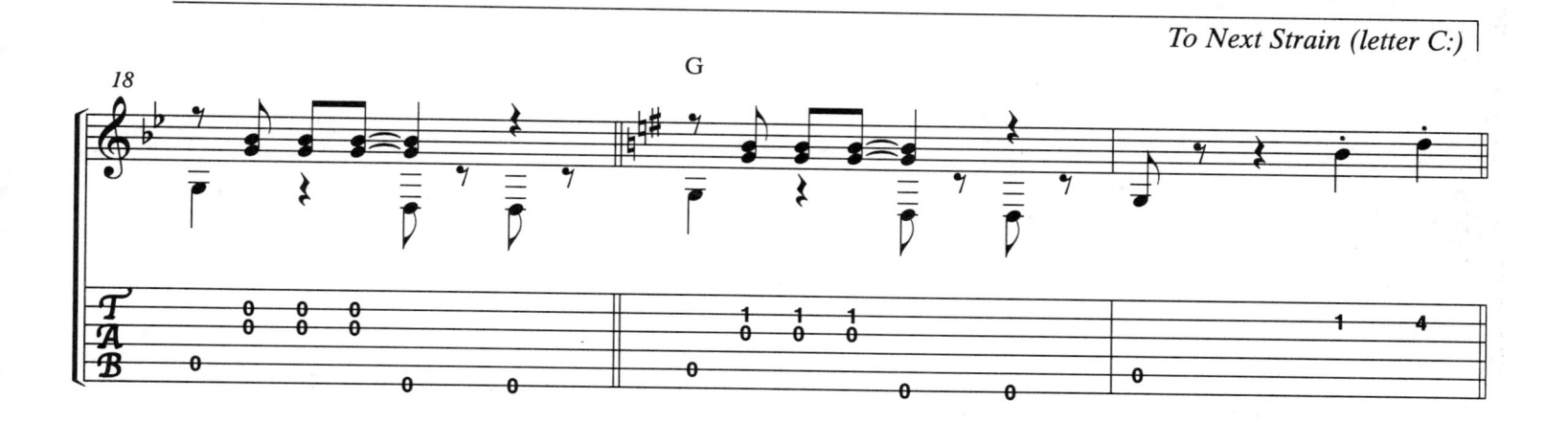

Siboney - 6 - 2
SAIR007

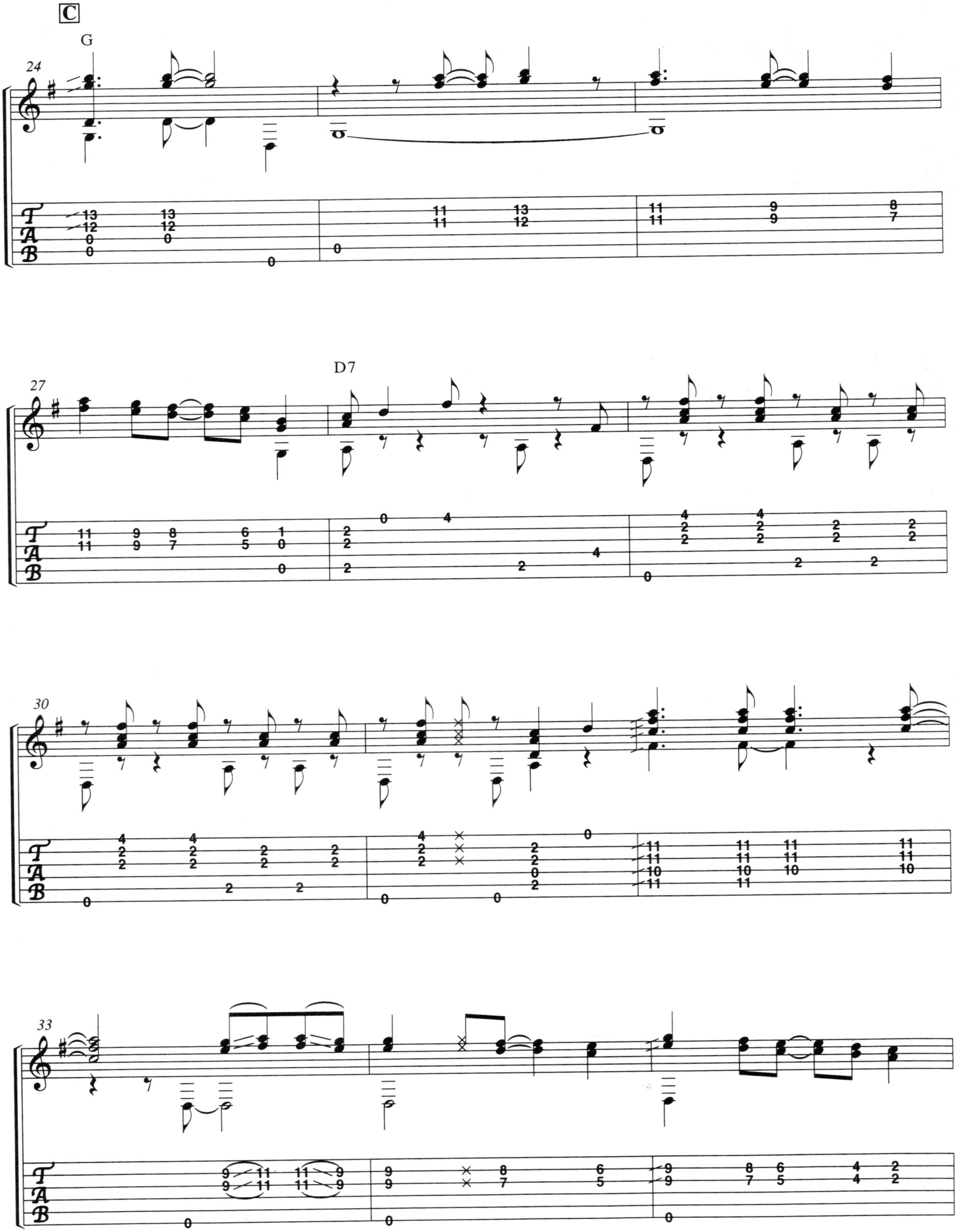
C
G
24
27
D7
30
33

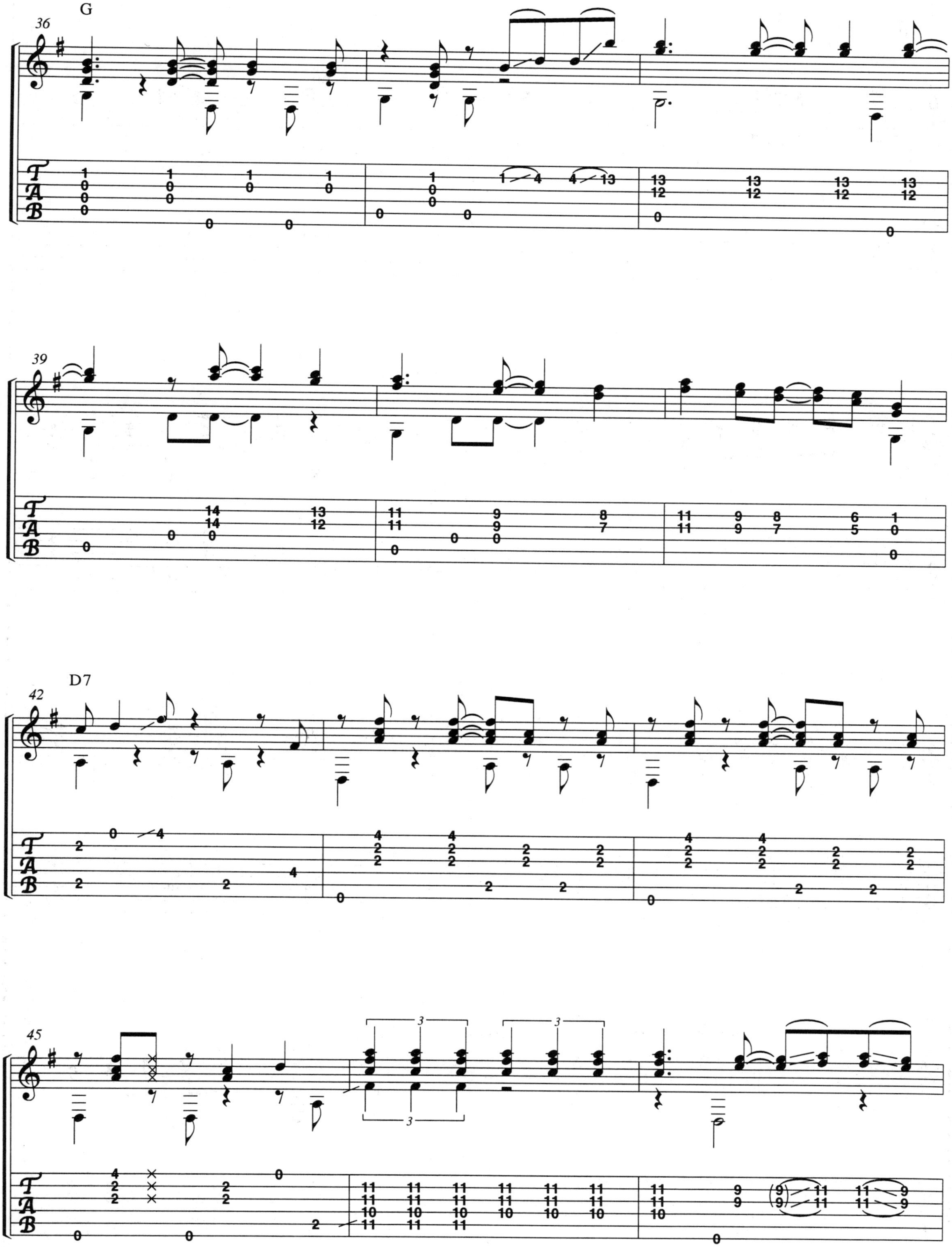
36
G
39
42
D7
45

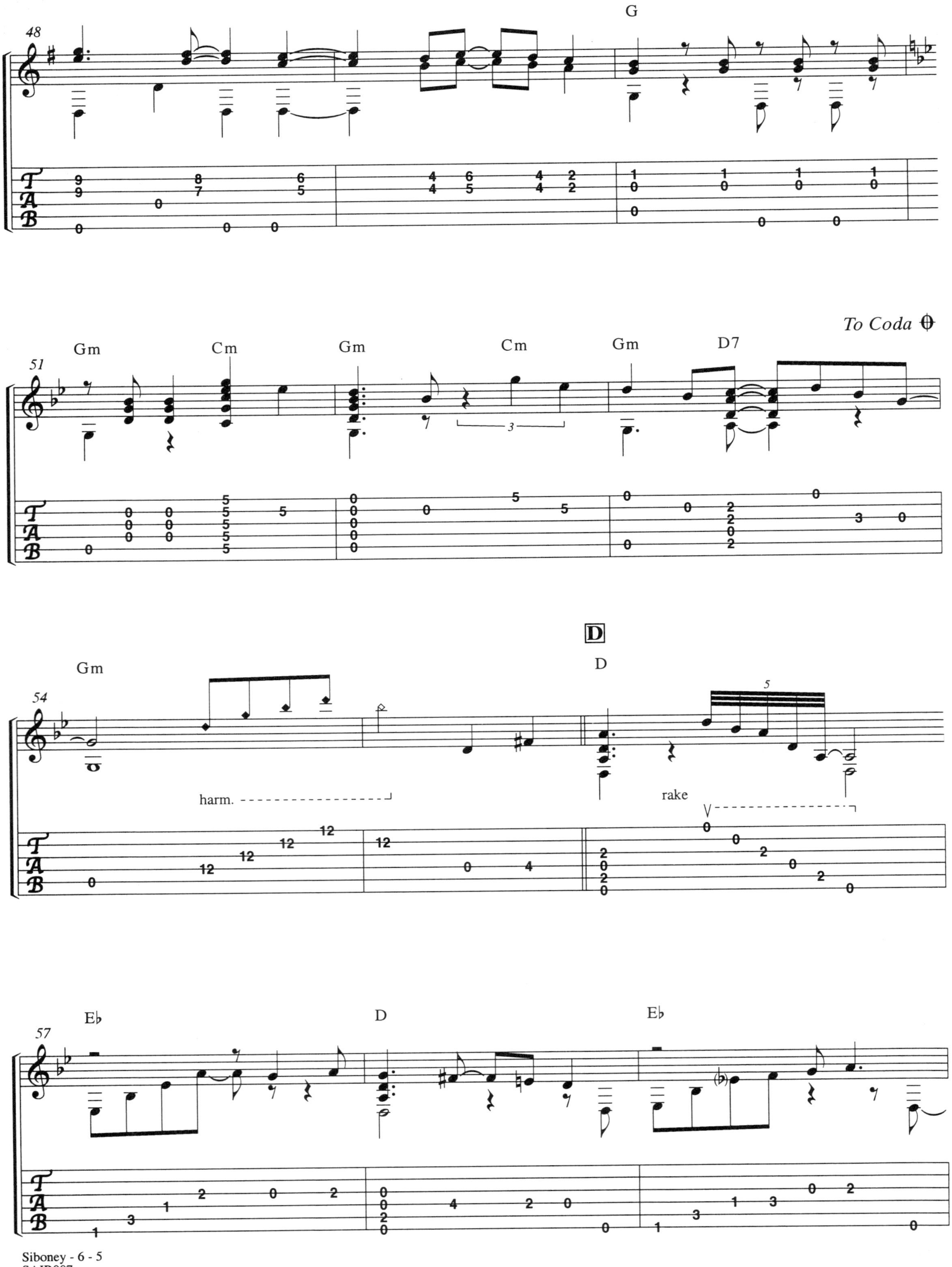
48
G
51
Gm
Cm
Gm
Cm
Gm
D7
To Coda
54
Gm
D
D
harm.
rake
57
E♭
D
E♭

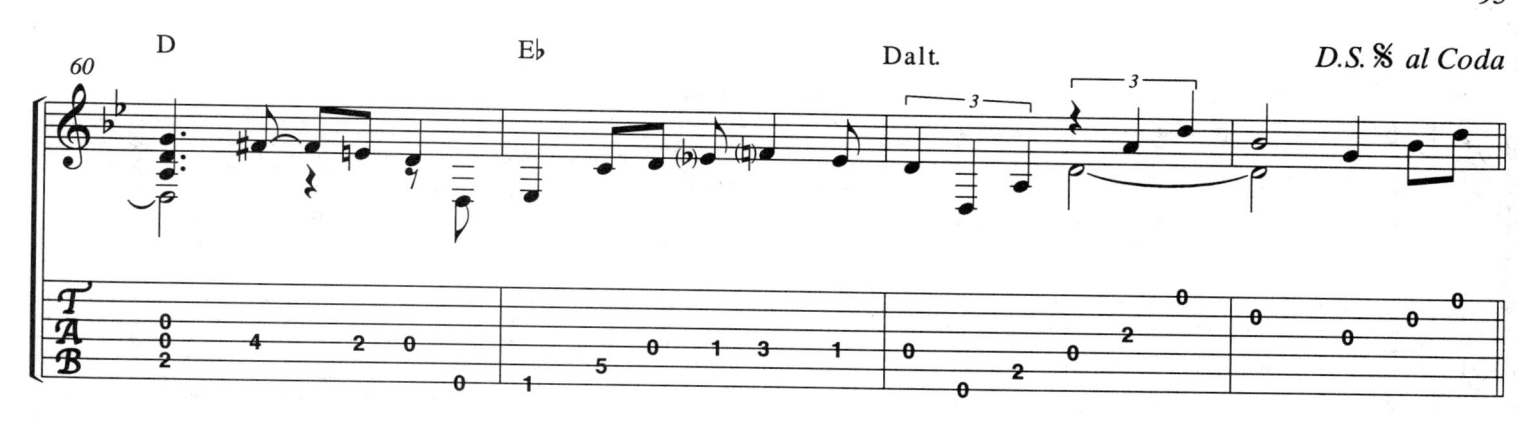

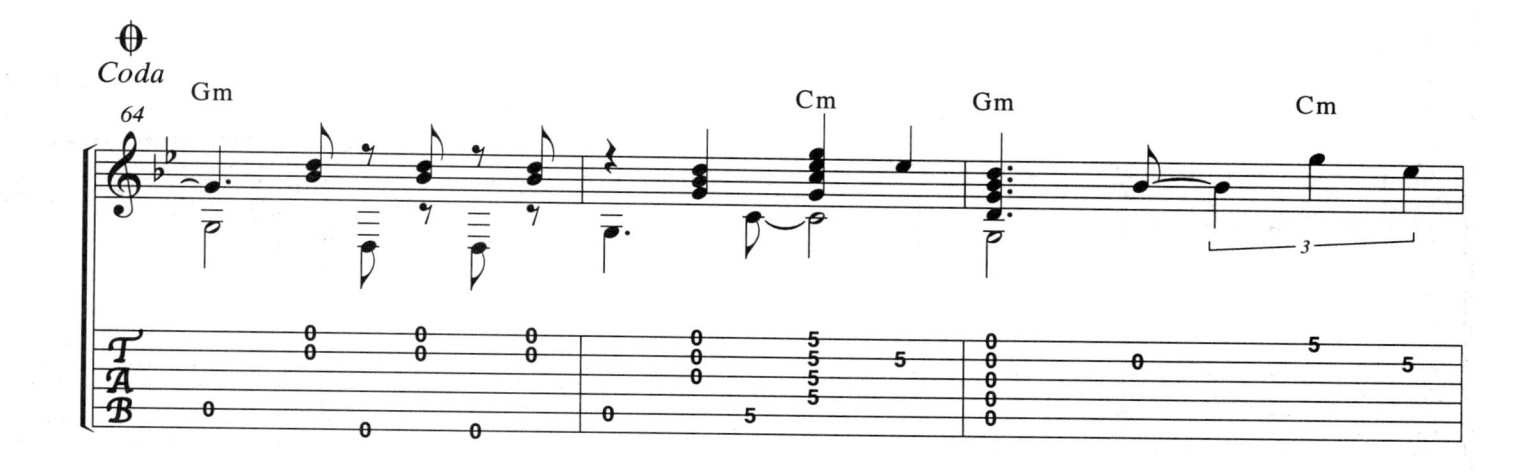

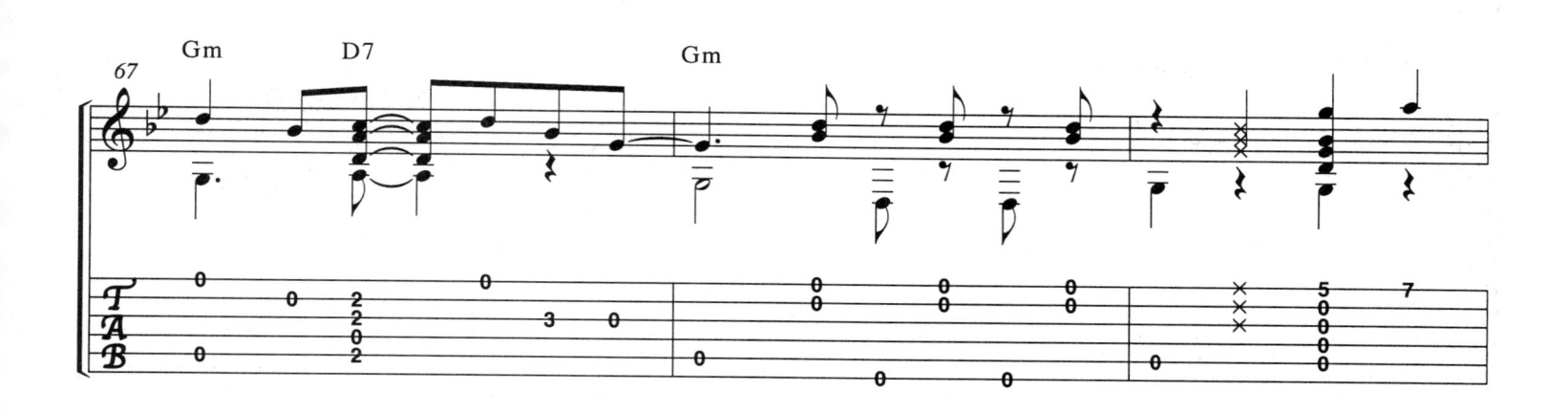

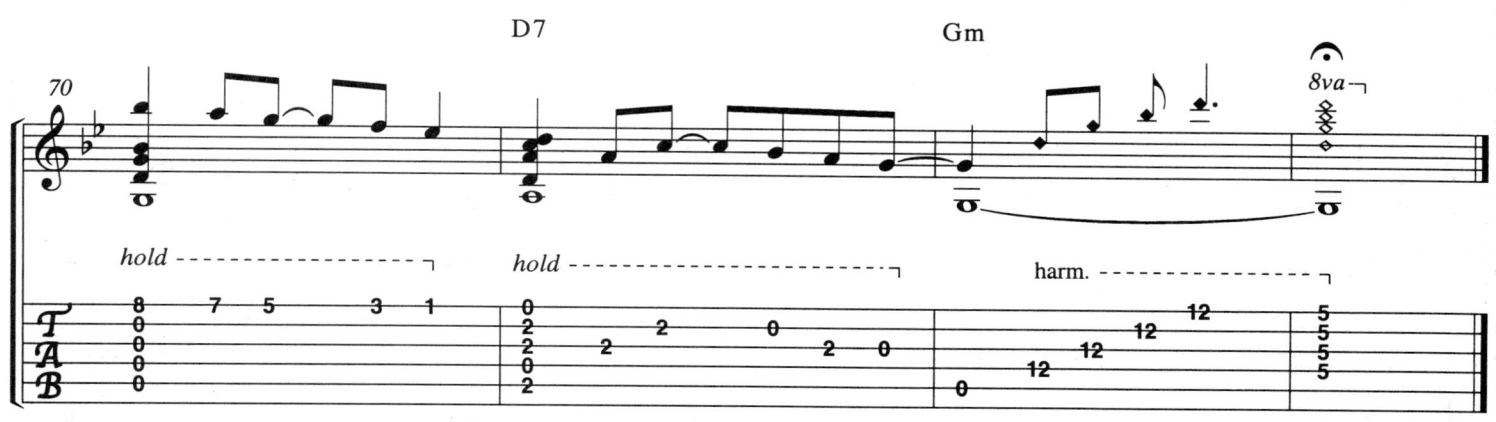

Siboney - 6 - 6
SAIR007

String Crazy

By MIKE DOWLING

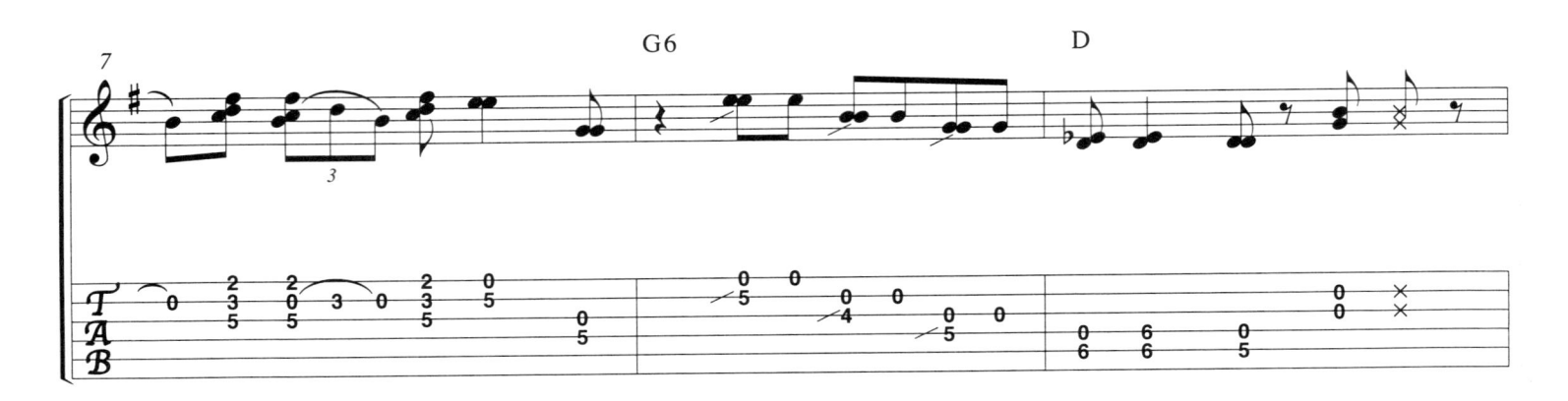

© 2000 TableTop Music (ASCAP)
All Rights Reserved

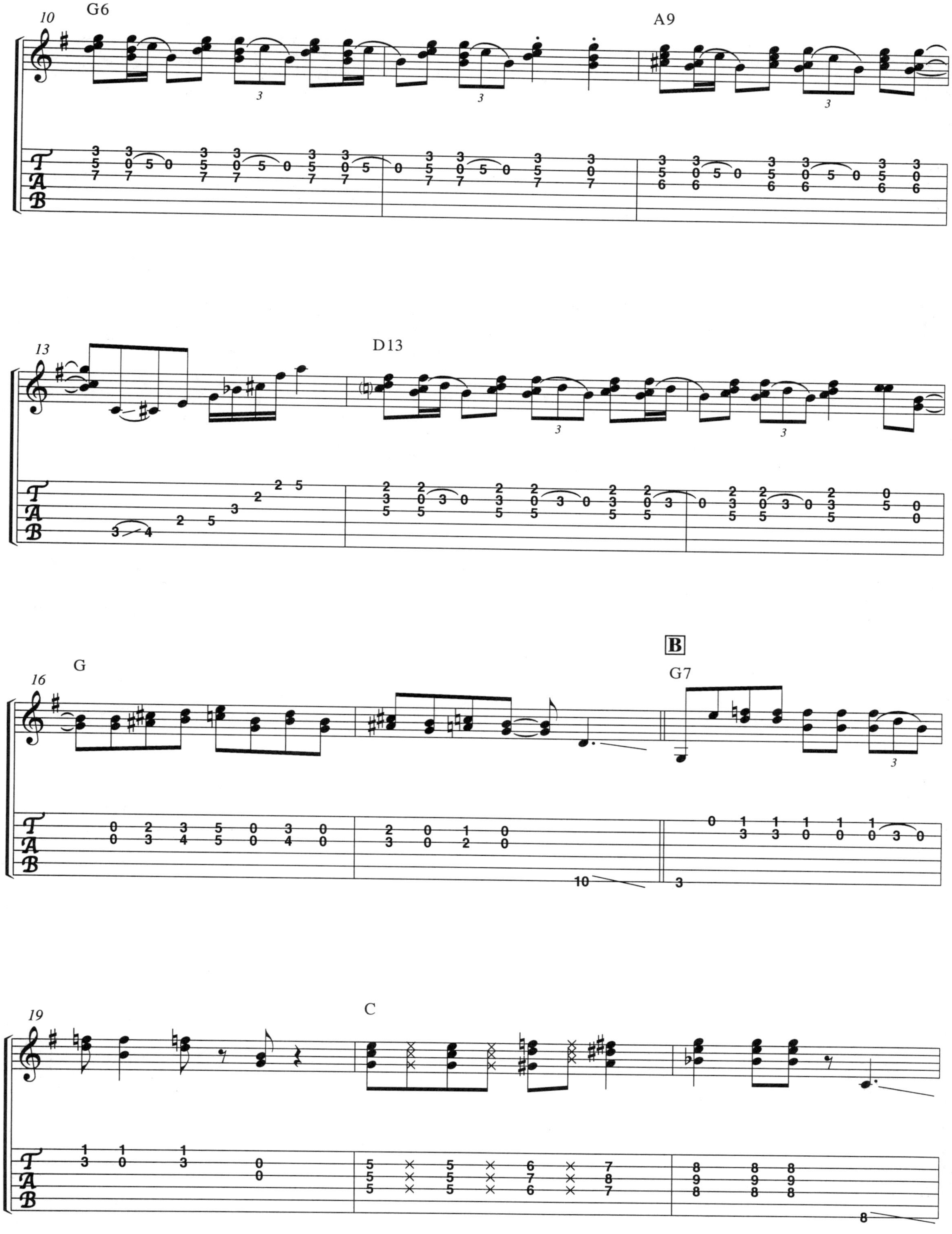
10
G6
A9
13
D13
16
G
B
G7
19
C

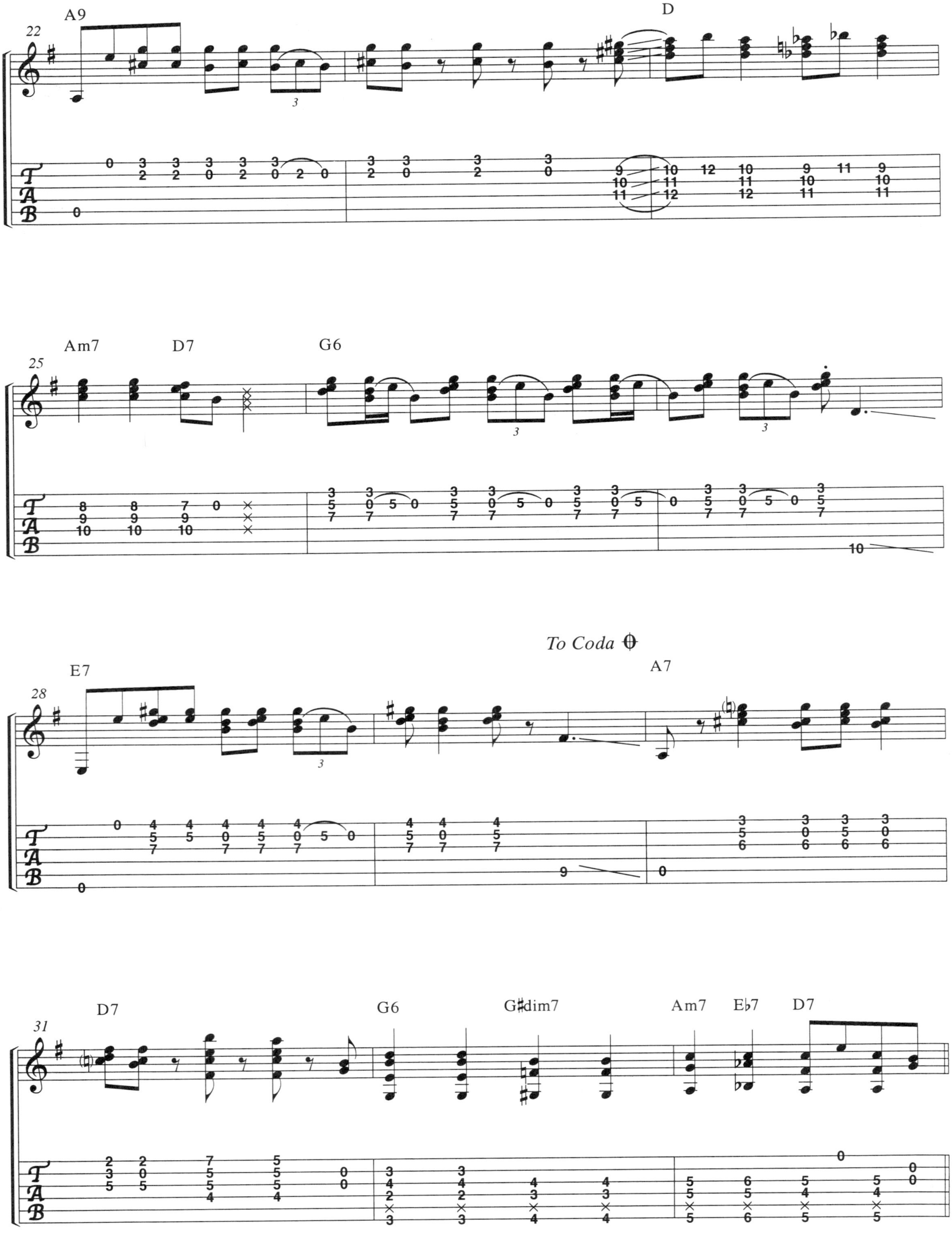
22
A9
D
25
Am7
D7
G6
28
E7
To Coda
A7
31
D7
G6
G♯dim7
Am7
E♭7
D7

String Crazy - 9 - 4
SAIR007

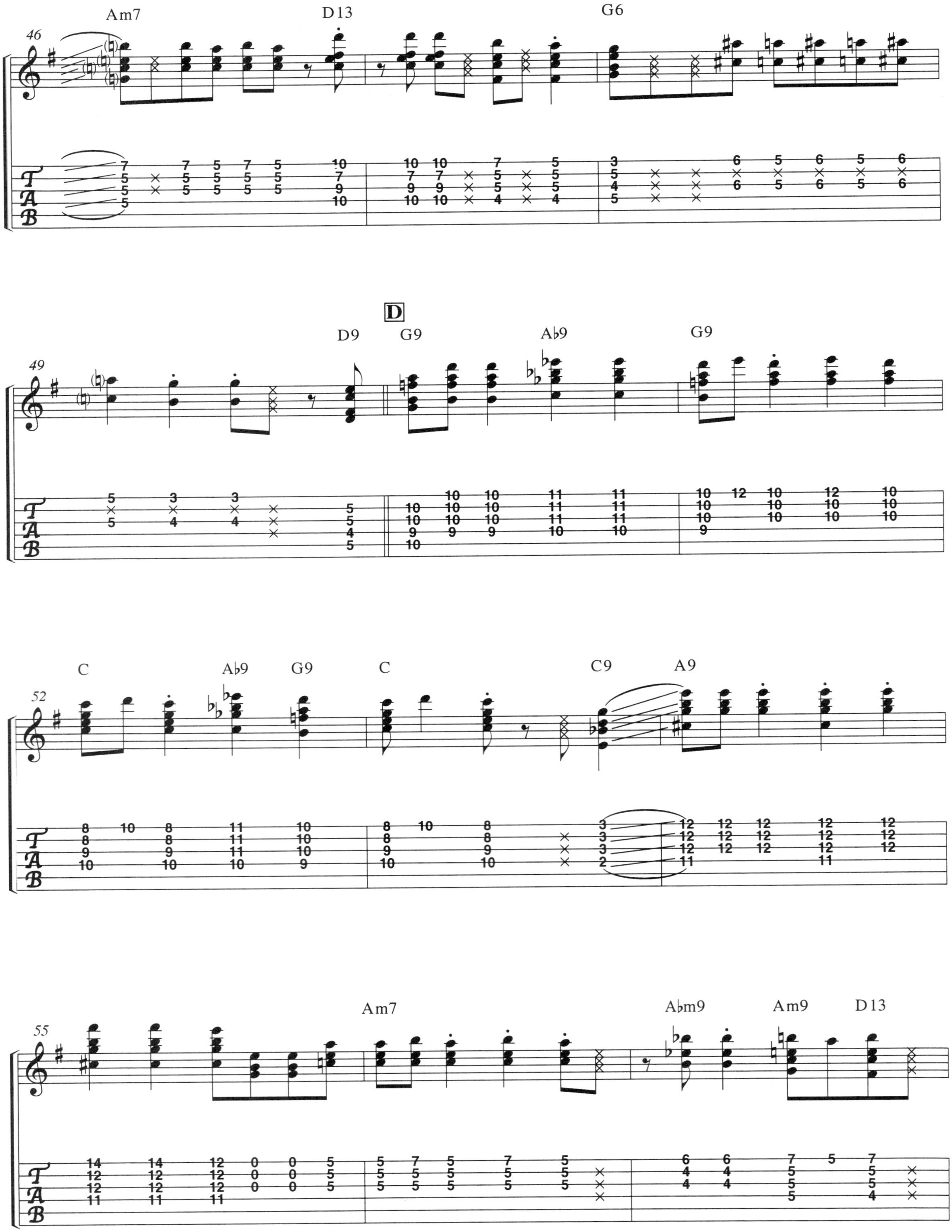
46
Am7
D13
G6
D
49
D9
G9
A♭9
G9
52
C
A♭9
G9
C
C9
A9
55
Am7
A♭m9
Am9
D13

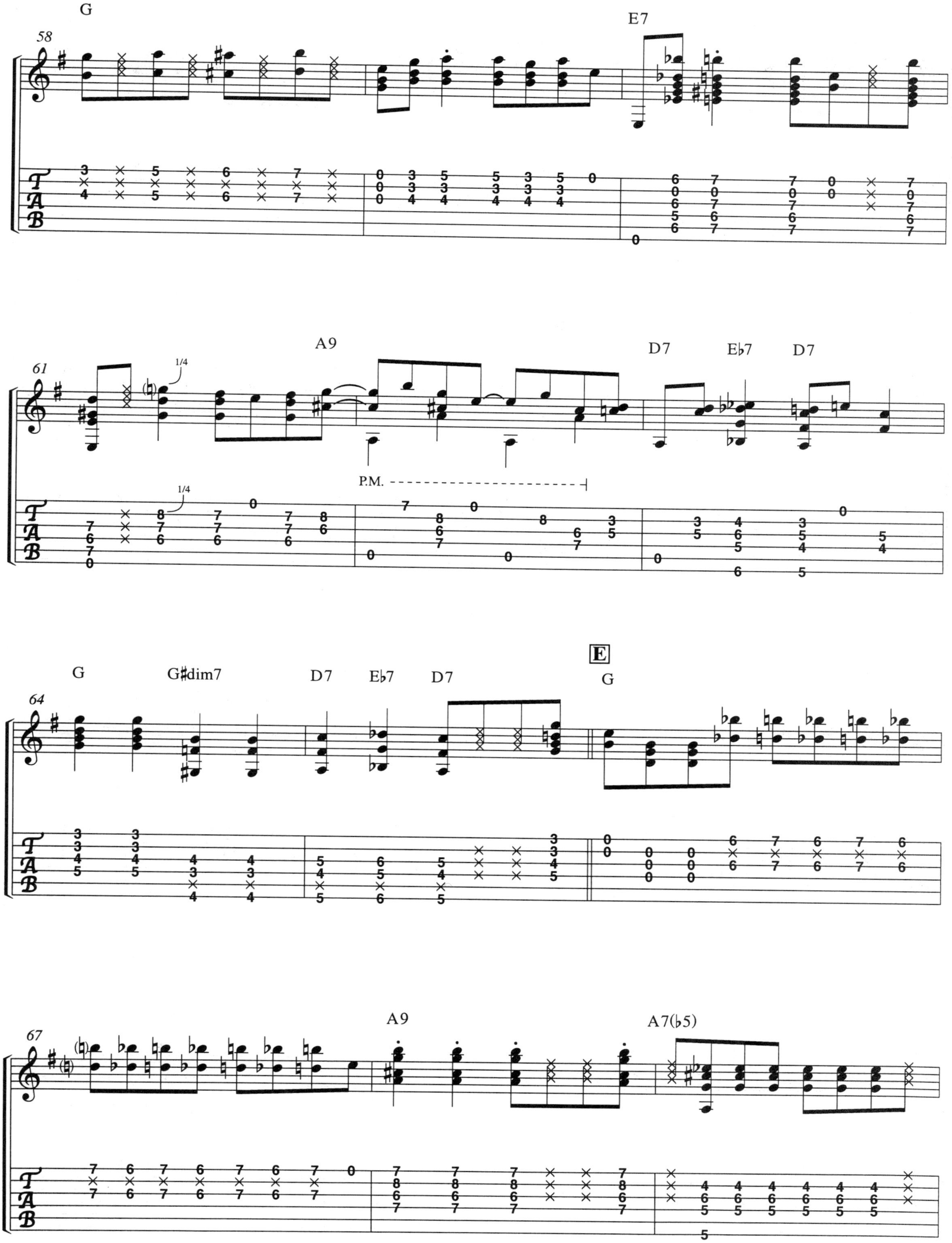
G
E7
A9
D7
E♭7
D7
1/4
P.M.
G
G♯dim7
D7
E♭7
D7
E
G
A9
A7(♭5)

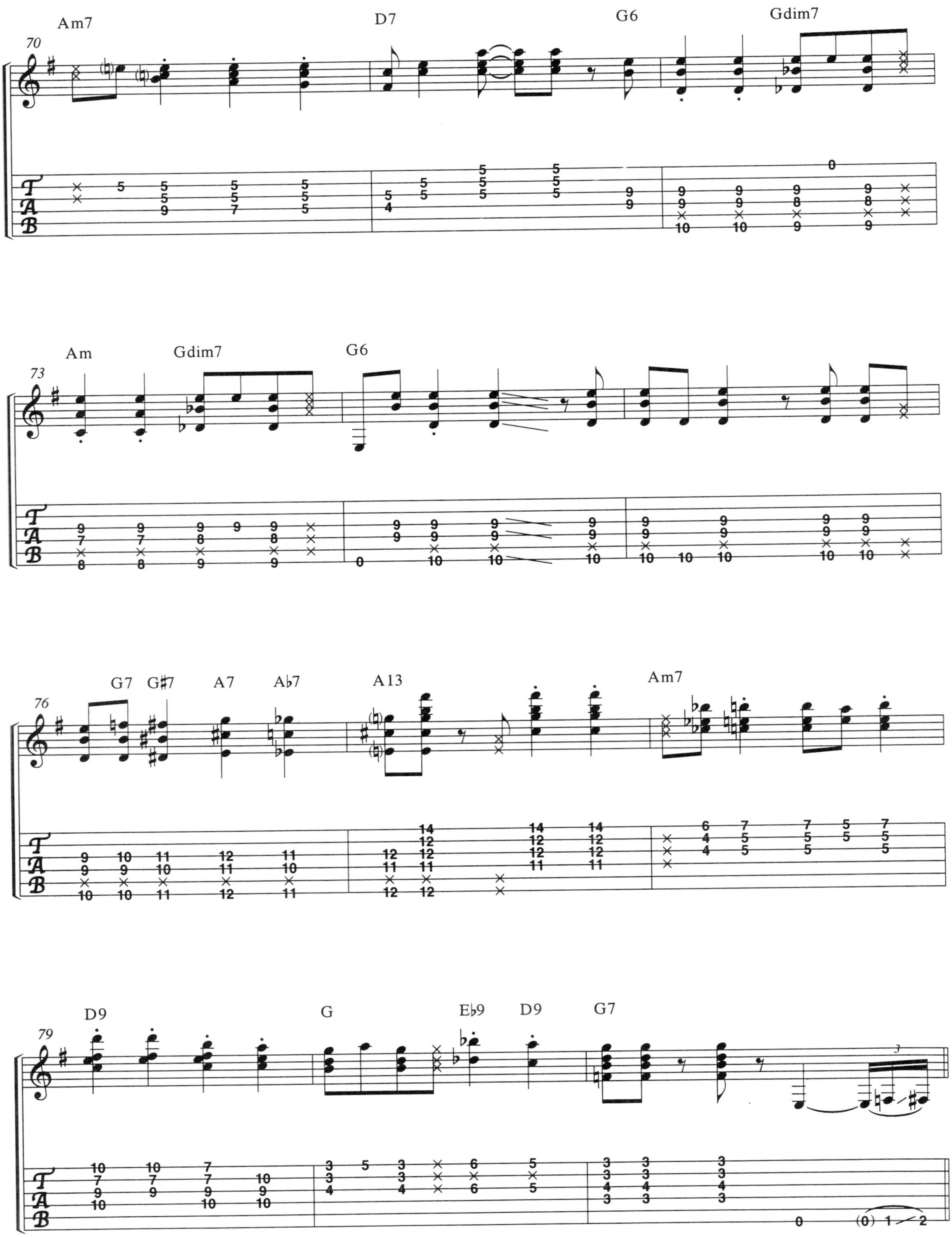
Am7
D7
G6
Gdim7
Am
Gdim7
G6
G7
G♯7
A7
A♭7
A13
Am7
D9
G
E♭9
D9
G7

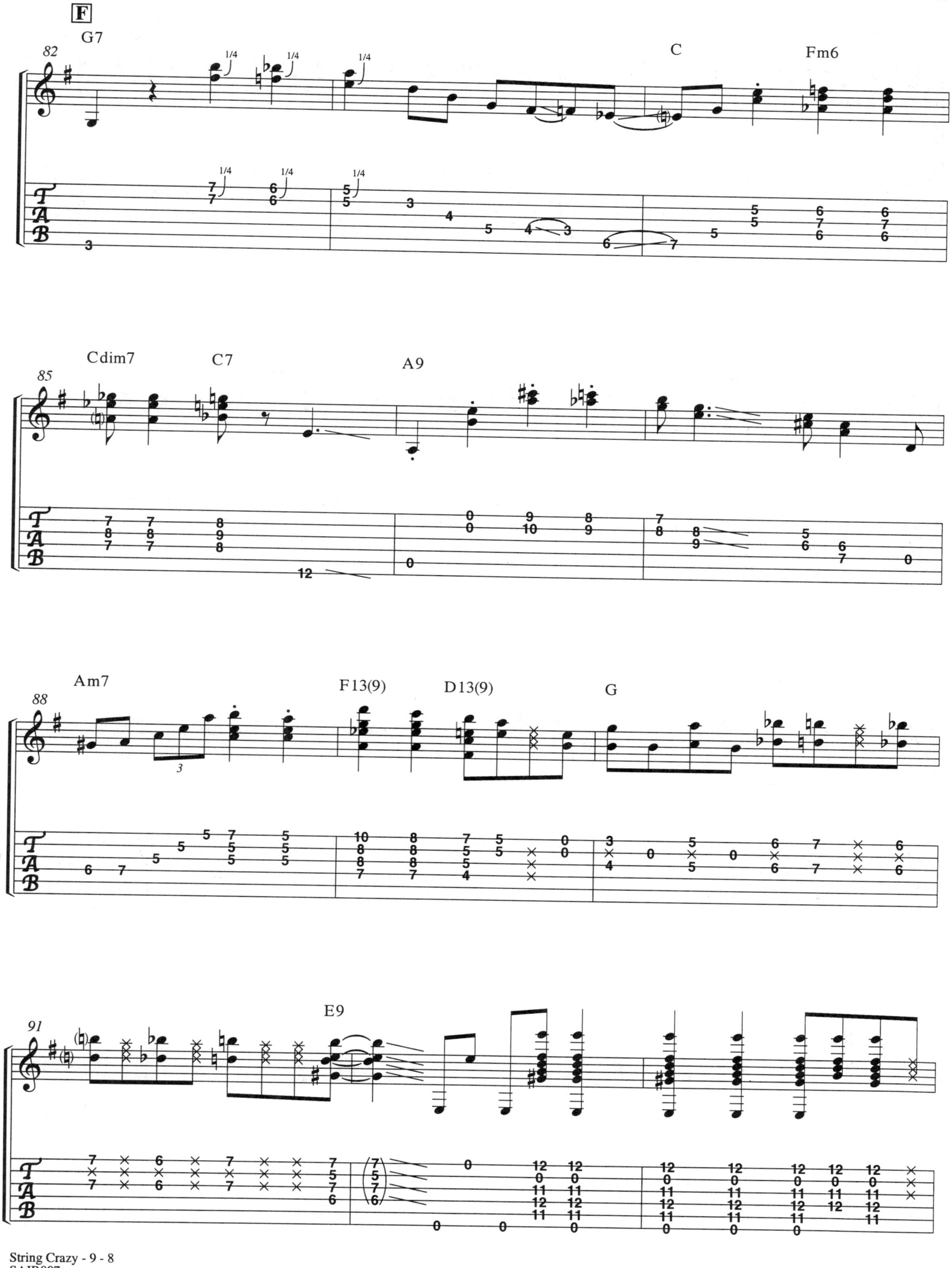
F
G7
82
C
Fm6
Cdim7
C7
A9
85
Am7
F13(9)
D13(9)
G
88
E9
91

String Crazy - 9 - 9
SAIR007

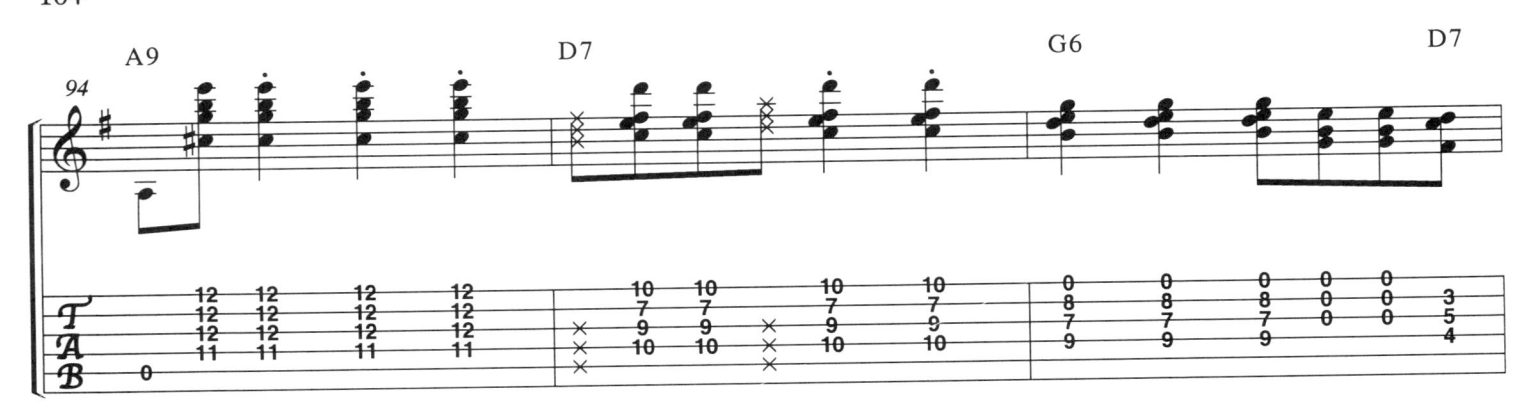

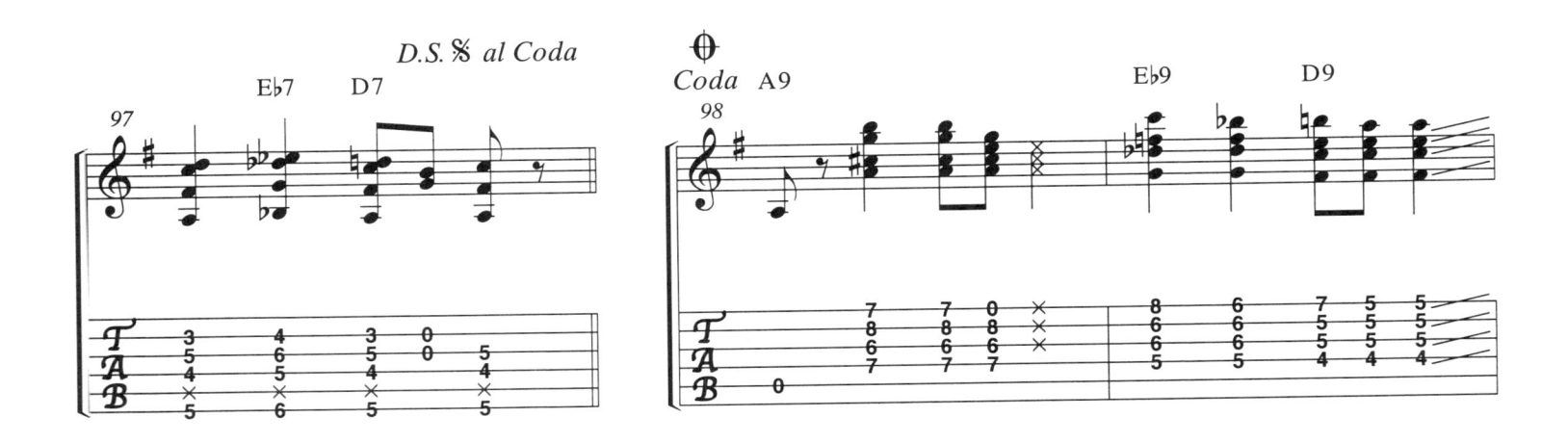

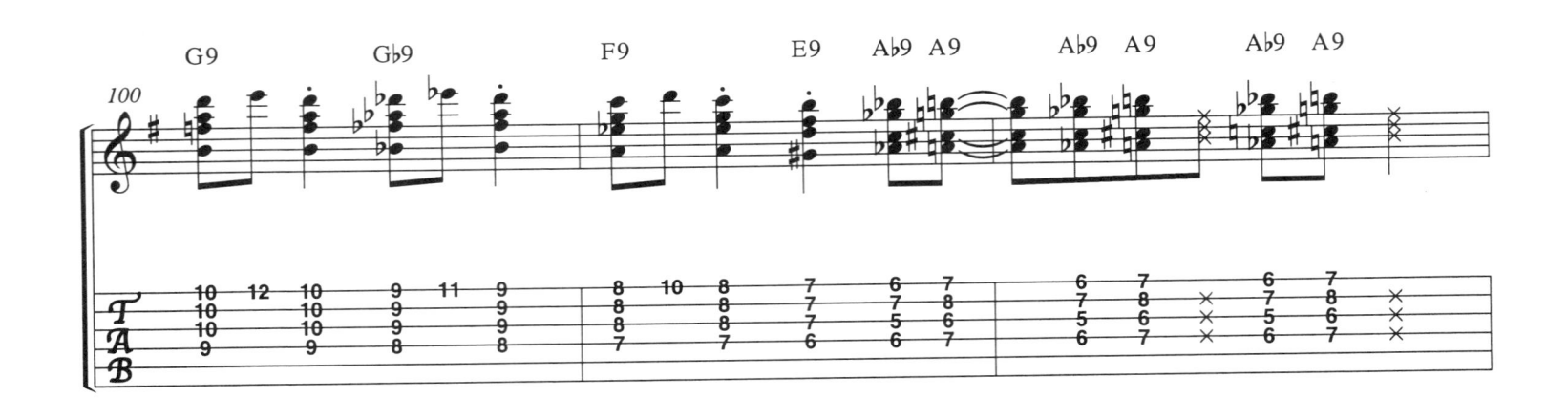

Swamp Dog Blues

By MIKE DOWLING

Open D tuning:
⑥ = D ③ = F#
⑤ = A ② = A
④ = D ① = D

Moderately (with a cut-time feel)

w/slide unless otherwise marked
let ring
w/o slide

Swamp Dog Blues - 5 - 1
SAIR007

© 1995 TableTop Music (ASCAP) and Solid Air Music (ASCAP)
All Rights Reserved

Swamp Dog Blues - 5 - 2

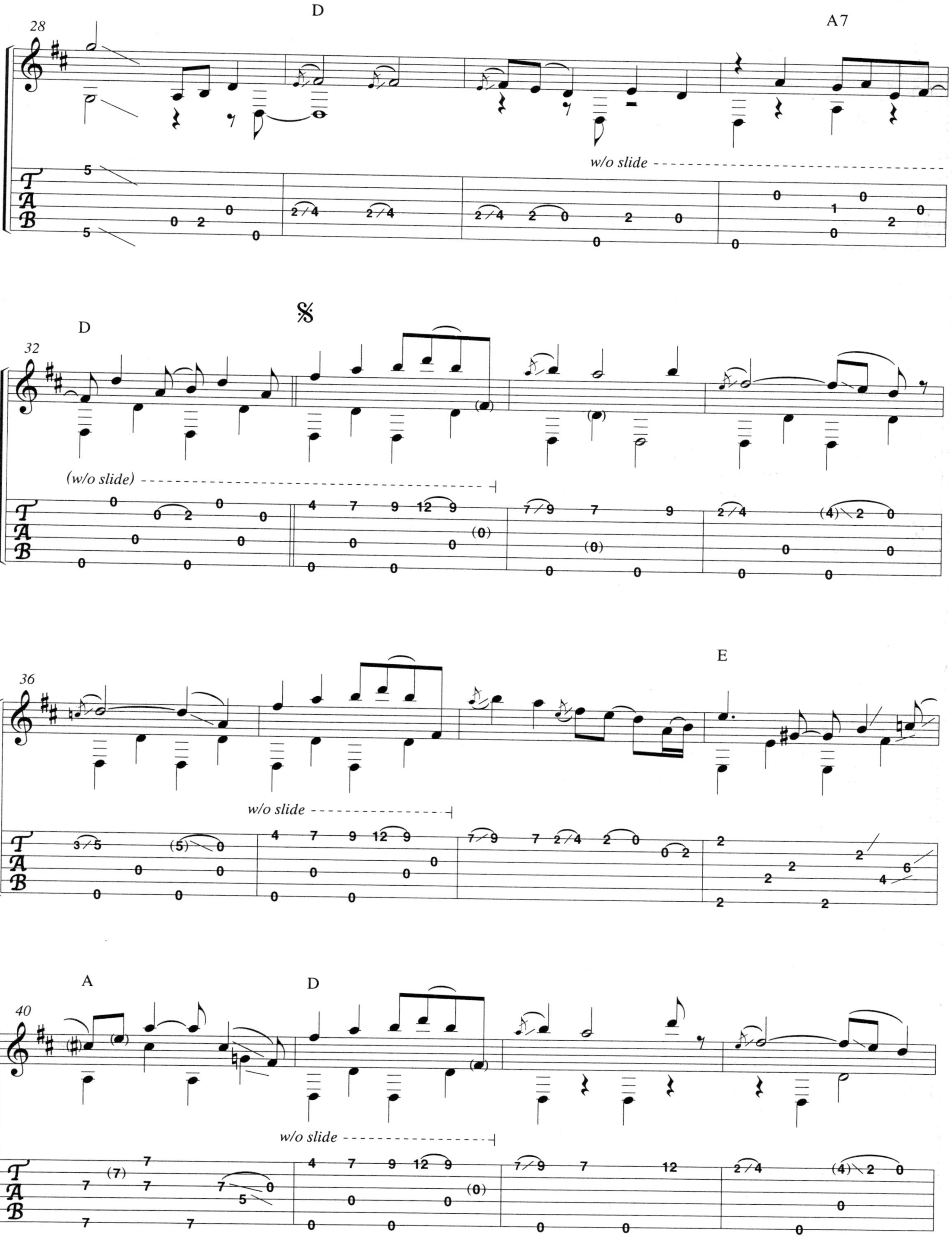
28
D
A7
w/o slide
32
D
(w/o slide)
36
w/o slide
E
40
A
D
w/o slide

44
F♯m Em D G D
1/2
w/o slide
48
To Coda
52
56
1/4
w/o slide
60
D
D.S. al Coda
(w/o slide)
w/o slide

Coda
D
A
8va
D
harm.
harm.
69
A
8va
D
harm.
harm.
w/o slide
73
G
77
D
G
D
1/2
81
D
G
D
1/2
w/o slide

Wild 'Bout It

By MIKE DOWLING

Open E tuning:
⑥ = E   ③ = G#
⑤ = B   ② = B
④ = E   ① = E

Moderately (cut-time feel)

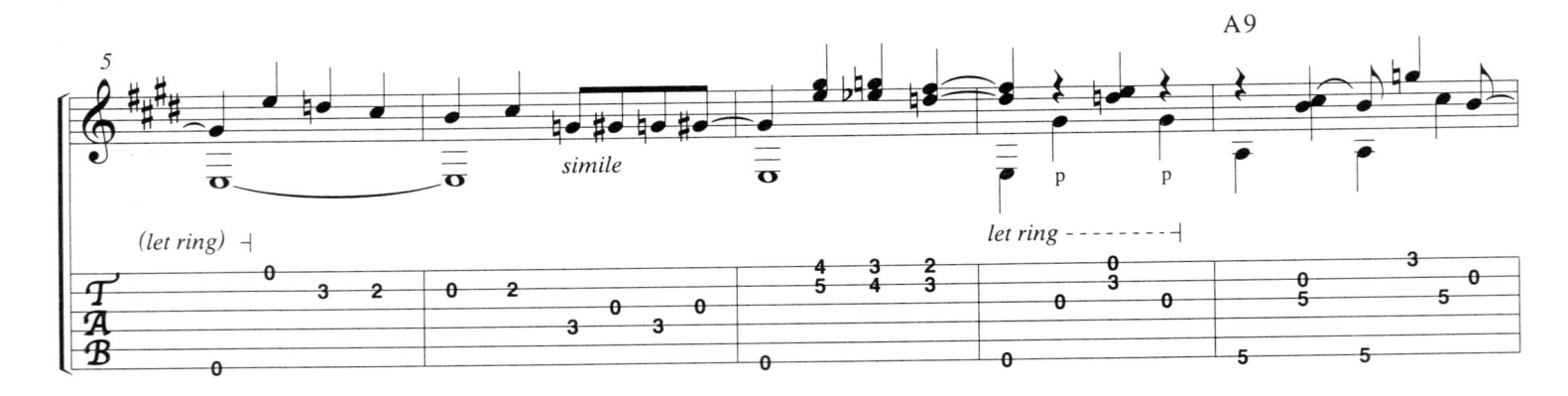

111

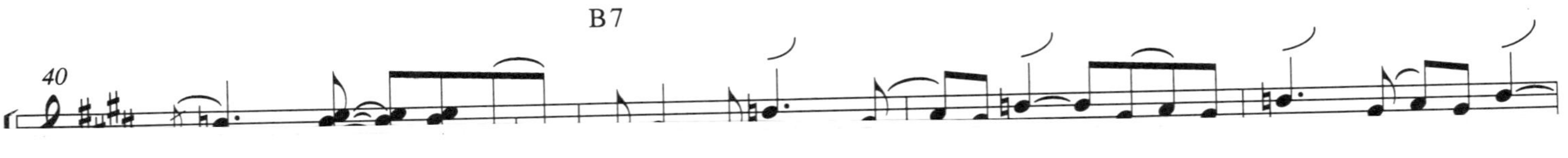

116

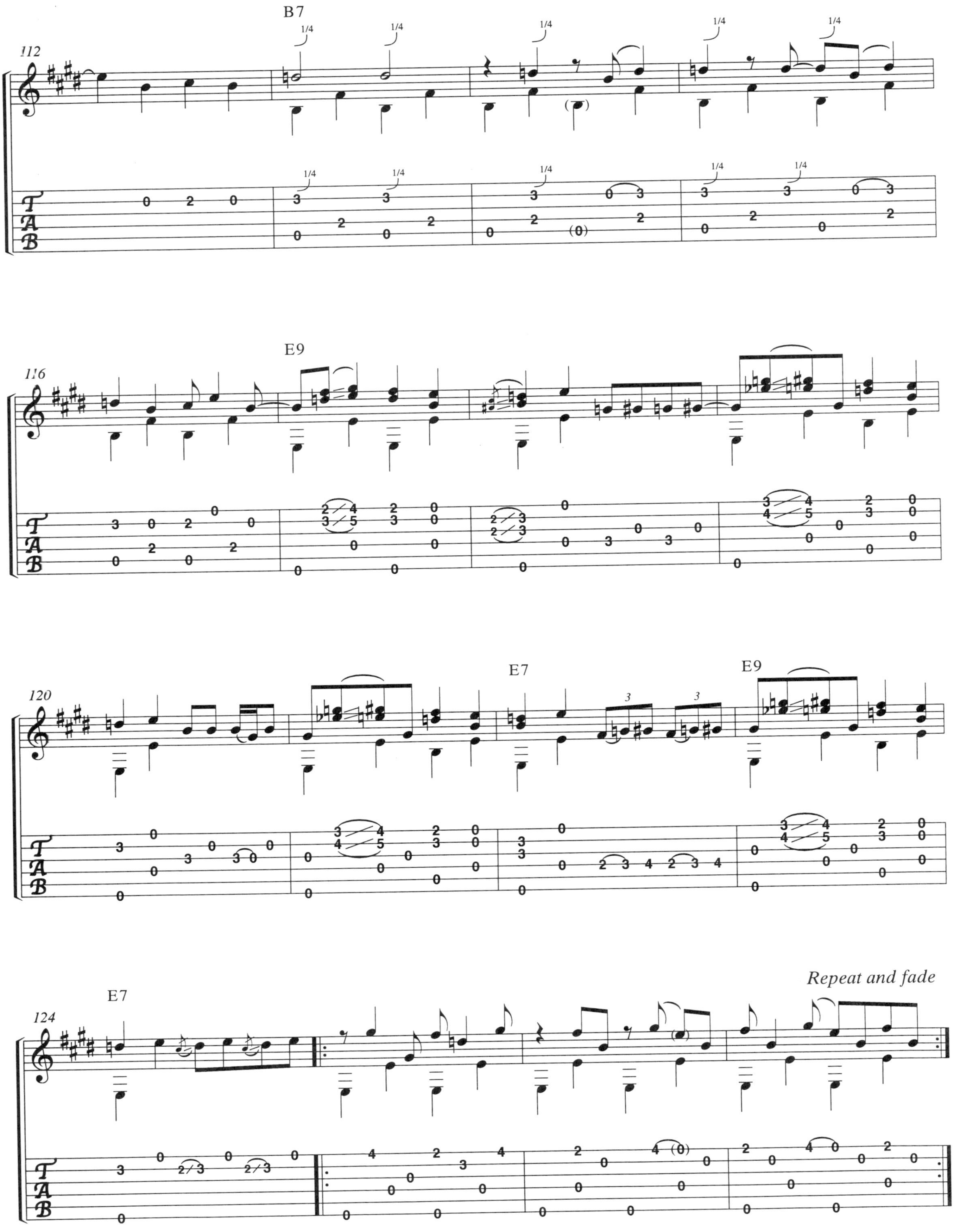

Discography

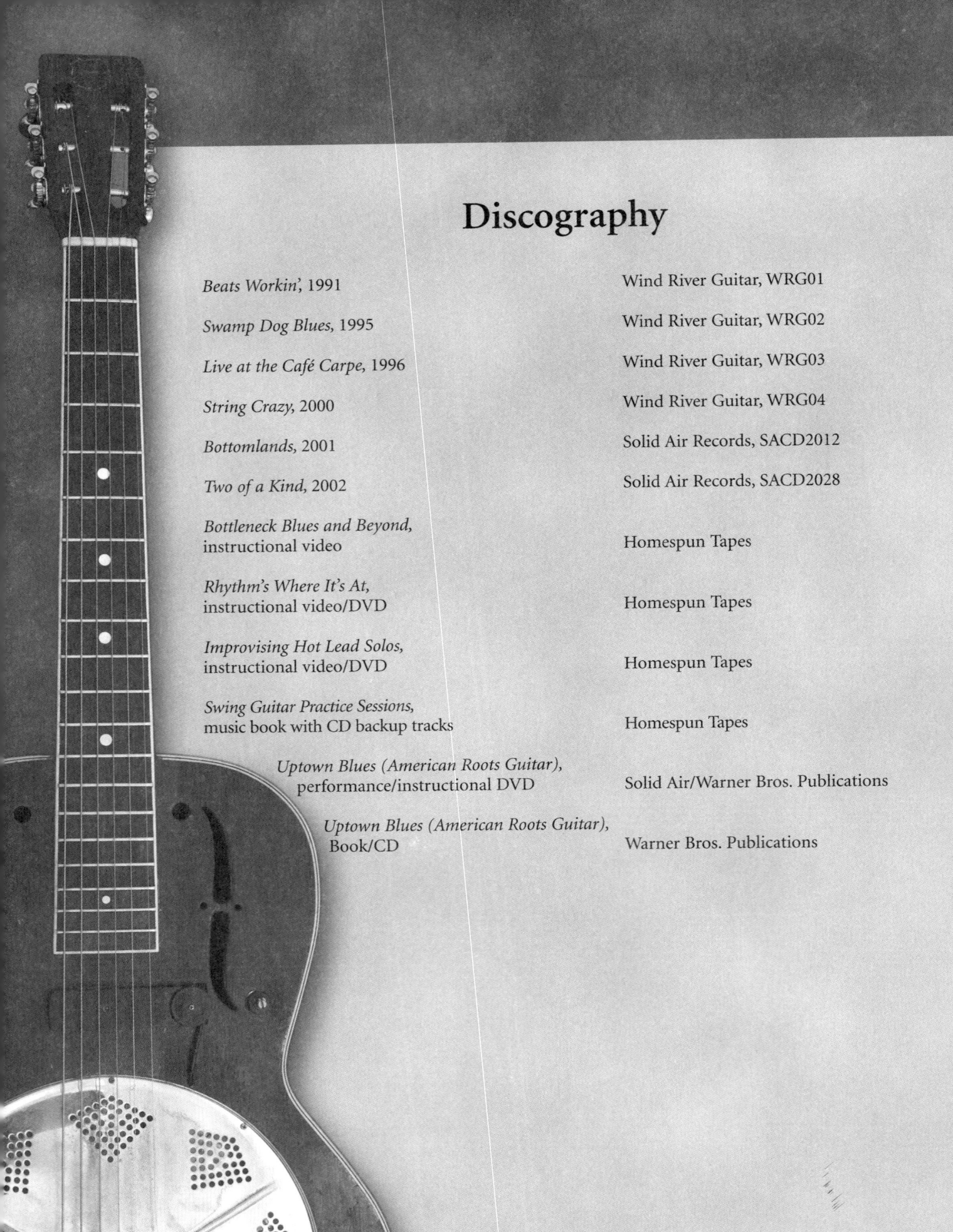

Beats Workin', 1991	Wind River Guitar, WRG01
Swamp Dog Blues, 1995	Wind River Guitar, WRG02
Live at the Café Carpe, 1996	Wind River Guitar, WRG03
String Crazy, 2000	Wind River Guitar, WRG04
Bottomlands, 2001	Solid Air Records, SACD2012
Two of a Kind, 2002	Solid Air Records, SACD2028
Bottleneck Blues and Beyond, instructional video	Homespun Tapes
Rhythm's Where It's At, instructional video/DVD	Homespun Tapes
Improvising Hot Lead Solos, instructional video/DVD	Homespun Tapes
Swing Guitar Practice Sessions, music book with CD backup tracks	Homespun Tapes
Uptown Blues (American Roots Guitar), performance/instructional DVD	Solid Air/Warner Bros. Publications
Uptown Blues (American Roots Guitar), Book/CD	Warner Bros. Publications

Mike Dowling

Guitarist

A professional career spanning four decades has taken Mike Dowling from sideman, session player, and bandleader to solo performer and composer of amazing versatility. Firmly grounded in authenticity and possessed of a musical soul as old as the vintage instruments he favors, Mike draws inspiration from deep in the musical bag of American roots guitar. Influenced by traditional Piedmont-style fingerpickers like Mississippi John Hurt and swing jazz legends like the late George Barnes, Mike has developed a style uniquely his own that he translates fluently to arch-top, flat-top, and resonator guitars. Early in his career, Mike caught the attention of mandolinist Jethro Burns, jazz violin great Joe Venuti, and master fiddler Vassar Clements. In the 1970s he worked and recorded with Burns and Venuti in Chicago and joined Vassar's first touring band for a stint on the road. Clements calls him simply "One of the finest guitar players there is, anywhere." Long respected among his peers as a truly "tasty" player, Mike can be heard on dozens of recordings, including Clements' 1979 Grammy-nominated *Nashville Jam*.

In 1995, after years of playing with various ensembles, Mike launched a solo performance career. Armed with an engaging voice, self-deprecating wit, and an arsenal of elegant interpretations of old blues, swing, ragtime, and original tunes, Mike quickly captured the hearts of acoustic music fans. With the release of his first solo album, the critically acclaimed *Swamp Dog Blues*, he began headlining at concerts and festivals throughout the world. In 1996, buoyed by his success as a soloist, Mike packed up his guitars and his fishing gear and moved from Nashville, Tennessee, to a little mountain town in western Wyoming. He and his wife opened Wind River Guitar and launched the Greater Yellowstone Music Camp for acoustic blues and swing instruction in the beautiful Grand Teton mountains. Mike continues to write and record from his Wyoming retreat and maintains a busy performance and teaching schedule. He has been a frequent guest on public radio's "A Prairie Home Companion," and his most recent release is an album of instrumental guitar duets recorded with PHC house band member Pat Donohue.

Mike welcomes student feedback and can be contacted through www.mikedowling.com.

Solid Air Records Presents
The Finest Acoustic Guitarists on DVD

Laurence Juber
The Guitarist
906729

The premier solo acoustic guitarist of our generation performs and explains six of his most popular solo guitar pieces in DADGAD and standard tuning.

David Cullen
Jazz, Classical and Beyond
906843

David Cullen's influences, which range from gospel to jazz and funk to classical music, combine to give him a unique voice and a deep sense of composition.

Doug Smith
Contemporary Instrumental Guitar
906842

With a background in classical guitar and composition and a rock band honored by *Musician* magazine as the finest in the country, Doug Smith brings these diverse influences to his contemporary instrumentals.

Kenny Sultan
Guitar Blues
906840

Kenny Sultan teaches six of his own compositions. These pieces serve as a virtual encyclopedia of blues licks and patterns.

Mike Dowling
Uptown Blues
906841

Mike Dowling performs a unique blend of blues, ragtime, swing, and roots music in standard and open tunings.

Al Petteway
Celtic, Blues and Beyond
906844

Al Petteway's compositions incorporate Celtic, blues, and R&B influences. Al also offers some great tips on how to color compositions with techniques that make the music sing.

Also Available as Books/CDs

Each book contains note-for-note guitar arrangements transcribed by the artists themselves in standard notation and tab. Plus, you get a masterclass-style CD on which the artist walks you carefully through the key aspects and techniques for each arrangement.

Laurence Juber:
The Guitarist Anthology, Vol. 1 (SAIR001)
The Guitarist Anthology, Vol. 2 (SAIR002)

David Cullen:
Grateful Guitar (SAIR003)
Jazz, Classical and Beyond (SAIR004)

Doug Smith:
Contemporary Instrumental Guitar (SAIR005)

Kenny Sultan:
Guitar Blues (SAIR006)

Mike Dowling:
Uptown Blues (SAIR007)

Al Petteway:
Celtic, Blues and Beyond (SAIR008)

AD1135 11/03